PREFACE

1. Scope

This publication provides doctrine for the command and control of joint maritime operations across the range of military operations. It also describes the maritime domain; addresses considerations for establishing a joint force maritime component commander and attendant command relationships; provides principles and guidance for the planning, execution, and assessment of joint maritime operations; and presents considerations for specific maritime operations.

2. Purpose

This publication has been prepared under the direction of the Chairman of the Joint Chiefs of Staff (CJCS). It sets forth joint doctrine to govern the activities and performance of the Armed Forces of the United States in operations and provides the doctrinal basis for United States (US) military involvement in multinational operations. It provides military guidance for the exercise of authority by combatant commanders and other joint force commanders (JFCs) and prescribes joint doctrine for operations, education, and training. It provides military guidance for use by the Armed Forces in preparing their appropriate plans. It is not the intent of this publication to restrict the authority of the JFC from organizing the force and executing the mission in a manner the JFC deems most appropriate to ensure unity of effort in the accomplishment of the overall objective.

3. Application

a. Joint doctrine established in this publication applies to the commanders of combatant commands, subunified commands, joint task forces, subordinate components of these commands, and the Services.

b. The guidance in this publication is authoritative; as such, this doctrine will be followed except when, in the judgment of the commander, exceptional circumstances dictate otherwise. If conflicts arise between the contents of this publication and the contents of Service publications, this publication will take precedence unless the CJCS, normally in coordination with the other members of the Joint Chiefs of Staff, has provided more current and specific guidance. Commanders of forces operating as part of a multinational (alliance or coalition) military command should follow multinational doctrine and procedures ratified by the United States. For doctrine and procedures not ratified by the United States, commanders should evaluate and follow the multinational command's doctrine and procedures, where applicable and consistent with US law, regulations, and doctrine.

For the Chairman of the Joint Chiefs of Staff:

CURTIS M. SCAPARROTTI
Lieutenant General, U.S. Army
Director, Joint Staff

- Added discussion of Navy's composite warfare doctrine.

- Added discussion of core maritime capabilities and missions.

- Added command and control considerations for specific maritime operations (surface warfare, air and missile defense, antisubmarine warfare, mine warfare, strike warfare, amphibious operations, naval surface fire support, information operations, maritime interception operations, maritime expeditionary security operations, maritime homeland defense, maritime operations threat response plan, counterdrug. noncombatant evacuation operations, protection of shipping, and foreign humanitarian assistance).

- Expanded the discussion on organizing the maritime force.

- Expanded the discussion of joint force maritime component commander responsibilities.

- Revised the discussion on boards, centers, and cells.

- Added discussion of support to an afloat joint force air component commander.

- Expanded the discussion of joint maritime support to multinational operations.

- Revised the discussion on logistic support to joint maritime operations.

- Added discussion of unmanned aircraft system.

- Removed the discussion on communications system support.

- Revised the discussion on movement and maneuver.

- Revised the discussion on maritime domain awareness.

- Modified the definitions for "aircraft carrier," "contiguous zone," "maritime domain awareness," "maritime power projection," "open ocean," prevention of mutual interference," "riverine operations," "sea control operations," "squadron," "theater antisubmarine warfare commander," and "undersea warfare."

- Removed the definitions for "antisubmarine warfare forces," "area operations," "at sea," "battle force," "defensive sea area," "force rendezvous," "general quarters," "marine environment," "maritime control area," "maritime supremacy," "nautical mile," "naval base," "on berth," "perils of the sea," "piracy," "riverine area," "sea surveillance," "service group," "service squadron," and "submarine patrol area."

• Assumed proponency for terms "antisubmarine warfare," "carrier air wing," "carrier strike group," "composite warfare commander," "numbered fleet," "officer in tactical command," "submarine operating authority," "surface action group," "surface combatant," "surface warfare," "task component," "task element," "task force," "task group," and "task unit."

• Added definitions of "forward presence," "global fleet station," "global maritime partnership," "maritime security operations," and "surface warfare."

TABLE OF CONTENTS

- **Describes Maritime Power, the General Approach to Command and Control, Maritime Capabilities and Missions, Interrelationship with Other Joint Operations, and the Maritime Domain**

- **Discusses Organizing for Joint Maritime Operations; to include Command Relationships and Responsibilities**

- **Explains Planning for Joint Maritime Operations**

- **Addresses Command and Control and other Operations Level Considerations for Specific Maritime Operations**

Introduction

Naval and maritime forces operate on (surface), under (subsurface), or above (air) the sea.

Maritime power, in the broadest sense, is military, diplomatic, and economic power or influence exerted through the ability to use the sea. The joint force commander (JFC) employs maritime power to influence events on land either directly through maritime power projection (e.g., amphibious assault) or indirectly through control and dominance of the maritime domain.

General Approach to Command and Control

Joint maritime operations (JMO) tend to be decentralized. The key tenets to command and control (C2) philosophy are the necessity of the subordinate commanders to execute operations independently but in accordance with a thorough understanding of the commander's intent, and command by negation or mission command.

Maritime Capabilities and Missions

There are five core capabilities of US naval forces: forward presence, deterrence, sea control, maritime power projection, and maritime security. Additional naval capabilities include: foreign humanitarian assistance (FHA), strategic sealift, seabasing, and homeland security support.

Interrelationship with Other Joint Operations

The degree of integration and coordination between joint force component commanders varies depending on the situation. For some JMO, the joint force maritime component commander (JFMCC) will likely operate without the support of other Service component forces whereas for others there may be detailed integration between components.

Maritime Domain

The maritime domain consists of the oceans, seas, bays, estuaries, islands, coastal areas, and the airspace above these, including the littorals. Maritime domain awareness (MDA) is the effective understanding of anything associated with the maritime domain that could impact the security, safety, economy or environment of a nation. Obtaining and maintaining accurate MDA is a key enabler of an active, and layered maritime defense in depth, and facilitates more expeditious and precise actions by the JFMCC and subordinate commanders.

Organizing for Joint Maritime Operations

General Organizational Options

Forward deployed maritime force packages are normally comprised of units that train together prior to deploying. These tailored force packages may include carrier strike groups (CSGs) and amphibious ready groups with an embarked Marine expeditionary unit. The JFC normally designates the forces and maritime assets that will be made available for tasking by the JFMCC, and delegates the appropriate command authority the JFMCC will exercise over assigned and attached forces and maritime assets made available for tasking. In cases where the JFC does not designate a JFMCC, the JFC may elect to directly task maritime forces.

Component Employment Considerations

When the JFC designates a JFMCC, the JFMCC's authority and responsibility are also defined by the JFC. The JFC may choose to conduct operations through a Service component commander or, at lower echelons, a Service force commander. This most often happens when there are no other Service or multinational maritime capabilities provided as part of the joint force; and the scope of operations along with the need for stability, continuity, economy, and ease of long-range planning dictate organizational integrity of Service forces for conducting operations.

Command Relationships and Responsibilities

JFMCC responsibilities for integrating JMO include, but are not limited to, planning, coordination, allocation, and tasking of JMO based on the JFC's concept of operations (CONOPS) and apportionment decisions. The JFMCC normally exercises operational control (OPCON) over assigned forces and OPCON or tactical control (TACON) over attached forces. Additionally, the JFMCC may exercise TACON over other military capabilities and forces made available for tasking. Specific responsibilities that normally are assigned to the JFMCC are:

- Develop a JMO plan.

- Provide centralized direction for the allocation and tasking of forces/capabilities made available.

- Make maritime apportionment recommendations to the JFC.

- Provide maritime forces to other component commanders in accordance with JFC maritime apportionment decisions.

- Control the operational-level synchronization and execution of JMO, as specified by the JFC.

- Assign and coordinate target priorities within the assigned area of operations (AO) by synchronizing and integrating maneuver, mobility and movement, fires, and interdiction.

- Coordinate the planning and execution of JMO with the other components and supporting agencies.

Organizing and Manning the Component Headquarters

The JFMCC's staff is typically built from an existing Service component, numbered fleet, Marine air-ground task force (MAGTF), or subordinate Service force staff and then augmented as required. In a maritime headquarters two complementary methods of organizing people and processes exist. The first is the doctrinal J-code structure, which organizes people by the function they perform (i.e., intelligence, logistics). The second is a cross-functional approach that organizes the staff into boards, centers, cell, and working groups that manage specific processes or tasks that do not fit well under the J-code structure and require cross-functional participation, such as targeting, assessment, and information operations.

Task Organization of Subordinate Forces

Each task force (TF) is assigned a commander, and only the commander reports to the JFMCC. The commander, task force (CTF), may further subdivide the TF into task groups, units, and elements to exercise control at the tactical level. These subdivisions may be organized based on capabilities, missions, geography, or a hybrid of all three.

Navy Composite Warfare Doctrine

The commander of a task organization is its officer in tactical command (OTC) when the organization is operating independently. The OTC can assign command functions to other commanders in the task component. This is the primary means by which commanders for each composite warfare functional areas are assigned. These warfare functional areas typically include surface warfare (SUW), air and missile defense, antisubmarine warfare (ASW), mine warfare (MIW), strike warfare, information operations (IO), and others as required. When multiple warfare functions are assigned, the OTC also designates a composite warfare commander (CWC) to coordinate overall operations. The OTC may choose to function as the CWC.

Multinational Considerations

Command authority for a multinational force commander (MNFC) is normally negotiated between the participating nations and can vary from nation to nation. Command authority could range from OPCON, to TACON, to designated support relationships, to coordinating authority.

Support to a Joint Force Air Component Commander Afloat

In operations where no shore-based air operations center (AOC) can initially be accommodated, the preponderance of capability to plan, task, and control joint air operations may be located afloat. This is most likely during the initial stages of forcible entry operations, cases where the US desires to limit the presence of forces ashore, or prior to the arrival of a shore-based AOC.

Planning for Joint Maritime Operations

Maritime Planning Processes and Products

The JFMCC's operational-level planning simultaneously supports the strategic and operational requirements of the JFC and also frames the tactical-level requirements of subordinate commanders. The JFMCC's planning is driven by the JFC's guidance and intent, supports JFC staff planning efforts, and should be closely coordinated with component planning. The JFMCC management mechanism is normally via operation orders (OPORDs), fragmentary orders, operation general matter, and operation tasks.

Integration with Joint Operation Planning Process

JFMCCs and their staffs not only contribute to the JFC's planning efforts but should also contribute to the development of other joint force components' supporting plans and OPORDs. Therefore, maritime staffs should be well versed in the joint operation planning process.

Organizing the Operational Area

Commanders and their staffs should assess friendly factors of space, time, forces, and degree of risk tolerance individually and then balance them in combination against the ultimate or intermediate objective. In harmonizing friendly operational factors against the respective objective, all considerations, when possible, should start with the quantifiable factors of space and time (i.e., operational reach).

Other General Planning Considerations

Other general planning consideration are: intelligence, fires and targeting, sustainment, C2 system support, environmental considerations, law of the sea, and unmanned aircraft systems.

Assessment

The maritime assessment group is responsible for establishing and updating the assessment picture in order to create a shared situational awareness among the staff, subordinates, and other components. These assessment snapshots support decision making through established battle rhythm events, such as battle or commander's update assessment type briefs, and make recommendations to either "stay the course" or change direction.

Multinational Participation

In a multinational environment, the operational aim for maritime forces is to exercise sea control, project power ashore, synchronize maritime operations with operations throughout the operational environment (OE), and support the MNFC's CONOPS, intent, and guidance in accomplishing the multinational task force (MNTF) mission. As with land forces, command of maritime operations will normally be assigned to a multinational force maritime component commander (MNFMCC) or a designated TF. The MNFC will typically assign a maritime AO to the MNFMCC or naval TF, based upon the CONOPS.

Command and Control and other Operational-Level Considerations for Specific Maritime Operations

The United States Navy's traditional and doctrinal warfighting configuration is the fleet, commanded by a numbered fleet commander.

Typically, the fleet commander task-organizes assigned and attached forces using the Navy's administrative organization as its foundation. The JFMCC may subdivide the maritime AO and create subordinate TFs, who may in turn create further subordinate organizations. In each case, the establishing authority must designate the command authorities for each subordinate organization, to include support relationships as required. Although the CTF is normally the CWC, the CTF can designate a subordinate commander to be the CWC. CTFs will typically assign forces under TACON to subordinate commanders.

Surface Warfare

SUW encompasses operations conducted to destroy or neutralize enemy naval surface forces and merchant vessels. These operations typically include the planning and directing of surveillance of the maritime domain, interdiction, and strikes by aircraft and missiles. SUW is conducted by the surface warfare commander (SUWC) and the strike warfare commander (STWC). The SUWC will be responsible for defense of the strike group against surface threats.

Air and Missile Defense

Specific to maritime operations is a self-defense zone (SDZ). An SDZ is a missile engagement zone around an individual surface-to-air capable ship, allowing the ship freedom to take defensive action. The maritime force benefits from and contributes to the joint air defense plan using shore-based and organic airborne early warning, fighter aircraft, ships armed with surface-to-air missiles, and electronic warfare systems.

The inner layer of defense for a maritime force is provided by a combination of point defense missiles, close-in weapons systems, and electronic countermeasures.

Antisubmarine Warfare

ASW is an operation conducted with the intention of denying the enemy the effective use of submarines. Undersea warfare (USW) operations are conducted to establish dominance in the undersea portion of the maritime domain, which permits friendly forces to operate throughout the OE and denies an opposing force the effective use of underwater systems and weapons. USW includes offensive and defensive submarine, antisubmarine, and MIW operations. The **theater ASW commander** is the commander assigned to develop plans and direct assigned assets to conduct ASW within the combatant command area of responsibility. The ASW commander [tactical-level] is responsible to the CWC for the defense of the force against submarine threats.

Mine Warfare

Maritime mine warfare (MIW) is divided into two basic subdivisions: the laying of mines to degrade the enemy's capabilities to wage warfare; and the countering of enemy-laid mines to permit friendly maneuver. In most cases, MIW operations are conducted under the framework of a TF architecture with the mine warfare commander or mine countermeasures commander reporting directly to the JFMCC.

Strike Warfare

Strike operations may employ ballistic or cruise missiles, aircraft, naval surface fires, Marines and special operations forces to attack targets ashore. The term "strike warfare" is used in the maritime domain and commonly includes joint fire support, interdiction, strategic attack, and close air support. The STWC is responsible to the CWC for planning, directing, monitoring, and assessing maritime power projection ashore and may be responsible for striking surface targets at sea at extended ranges from the strike group.

Amphibious Operations

Amphibious operations are complex and normally involve all components of the joint force. The JFC and JFMCC should ensure that the amphibious objective area or operational area is shaped by CSGs and other maritime and joint assets in anti-access/area denial environments prior to the commencement of the amphibious operation.

Naval Surface Fire Support

Naval surface fire support (NSFS) units are normally OPCON to the Navy component commander or TACON to the JFMCC and provide direct or general support to other joint force components or subordinate forces of the JFMCC (e.g., an amphibious force). When supporting a landing force or other ground forces, a NSFS spotting team is usually attached to the maneuvering forces for fire support coordination purposes.

Maritime Interception Operations

Maritime interception operations (MIO) are efforts to monitor, query, and board merchant vessels in international waters to enforce sanctions against other nations such as those in support of United Nations Security Council resolutions and/or prevent the transport of restricted goods. MIO lines of authority should be streamlined, and must be clearly understood by all forces involved in the conduct of the mission.

Maritime Security Operations

Maritime security includes a collection of tasks that are derived from agreed-upon international law. Maritime security operations are those operations conducted to assist in establishing the conditions for security and protection of sovereignty in the maritime domain.

Maritime Expeditionary Security Operations

A maritime expeditionary security force (MESF) is organized as an adaptive security force package supporting the JFMCC in providing all-weather, day and night security in the transition from the sea base inland, green to brown water, and ashore. The maritime expeditionary security force commander is that officer designated to conduct MESF operations within a designated coastal geographic area.

Seabased Operations

A sea base provides a JFC with a scalable and mobile capability in the joint operations area from which to exercise C2 or provide strike, power projection, fire support, and logistics capabilities where and when needed. A sea base can be as small as one ship, or it can expand to consist of dozens of ships. During any operation, merchant ship activity needs to be closely monitored, and effective coordination and close cooperation between military, civilian, commercial, and government organizations is required to provide for the necessary level of liaison and safety.

Protection of Shipping

There are multiple methods and options to protect shipping. One method is to conduct wide sea control operations that attempt to protect the waters or known traffic routes through which many ships pass. Another method is to gather merchant ships and devote protection assets to the convoy, requiring only localized supremacy.

Maritime Pre-Positioning Force Operations

A maritime pre-positioning force operation includes the airlift of MAGTF and Navy elements, the Navy support element, and naval port security units with selected equipment into an arrival and assembly area to join with equipment and supplies carried aboard maritime pre-positioning ships.

Other Operational-Level Considerations for Specific Maritime Operations

Other operational-level considerations for specific maritime operations include: IO, maritime homeland defense, defense support of civil authorities, maritime operational threat response plan, global maritime partnerships, security cooperation, global fleet stations; counterdrug operations; noncombatant evacuation operations, and FHA.

CONCLUSION

This publication provides doctrine for the C2 of JMO across the range of military operations. It also describes the maritime domain; addresses considerations for establishing a JFMCC and attendant command relationships; provides principles and guidance for the planning, execution, and assessment of JMO; and presents considerations for specific maritime operations.

Intentionally Blank

CHAPTER I
INTRODUCTION

"Whosoever can hold the sea has command of everything."

Themistocles (524-460 B.C.)
Athenian Politician and General

1. General

a. The terms "naval" and "maritime" forces are used throughout this publication to encompass Navy, Marine Corps, and United States Coast Guard (USCG) personnel, weapon systems, and organizations. Naval and maritime forces operate on (surface), under (subsurface), or above (air) the sea.

b. The maritime domain consists of the oceans, seas, bays, estuaries, islands, coastal areas, and the airspace above these, including the littorals. Nothing in the definitions of, or the use of the term domain, implies or mandate exclusivity, primacy, or command and control (C2) of that domain.

c. Maritime power, in the broadest sense, is military, diplomatic, and economic power or influence exerted through the ability to use the sea. The joint force commander (JFC) employs maritime power to influence events on land either directly through maritime power projection (e.g., amphibious assault) or indirectly through control and dominance of the maritime domain. Maritime power provides the JFC with many unique advantages:

(1) Maritime forces provide a means of maintaining a global, persistent military presence while limiting the undesired economic or diplomatic repercussions that often accompany US forces based ashore.

(2) Movement and maneuver of forces within international waters can take place without prior diplomatic agreement.

(3) Due to the reduced presence of civilians and infrastructure on or under the water, there is a reduced risk of friendly fire or collateral damage. While this is true on the open seas, there is significant civilian maritime traffic in coastal and littoral areas as well as in ports. In these areas risk of civilian casualties and collateral damage remains significant.

(4) Maritime forces are mostly a self-deploying, self-sustaining, sea-based expeditionary force and a combined-arms team, tailored to conduct operations across the range of military operations. Maritime forces are manned, trained, and equipped to operate with limited reliance on ports or airfields.

d. This publication provides joint doctrine for the C2 of joint maritime operations (JMO) and discusses the responsibilities of a joint force maritime component commander (JFMCC). Maritime operations include any actions performed by maritime forces to gain or exploit command of the sea, sea control, sea denial, or to project power from the sea. Sea control may include naval cooperation and guidance for shipping (NCAGS), protection of sea lines of communications (SLOCs), air lines of communications (ALOCs), blockades, embargoes against economic or military shipping, and maritime interception operations (MIO). Maritime operations also encompass operations to locate, classify, track, and target surface vessels, submarines, and aircraft. In addition, amphibious operations, as a form of power projection, increase the commander's options for maneuver in the littorals and forcible entry operations.

e. Maritime forces participate in operations ashore through the projection of power. They can execute, support, or enable missions ashore by conducting forcible entry operations (such as an amphibious raid or assault), seabasing of assets, moving land forces into the operational area via sealift, providing fire and air support, and influencing operations through deterrence. Maritime forces also may be employed in littoral waters for the conduct of sea control or denial, ballistic missile defense (BMD), and support joint force or component C2 platforms. Joint forces can support maritime operations with surveillance, logistics, fires and air support, and military engineering.

f. Effective C2 of maritime operations is complex, due to the requirement to operate continuously in the physical domains and information environment, and by the multi-mission nature of most maritime platforms. The flexibility, mobility, lethality, persistence, and speed of maritime forces, together with the expanse and unique characteristics of the maritime domain, present both opportunities and challenges to the JFMCC. The adversary also may choose to exploit the advantages of the maritime domain, but they will face the same challenges.

2. General Approach to Command and Control

a. C2 of maritime forces is shaped by the characteristics and complexity of the maritime domain, and the traditions and independent culture of maritime forces. The key tenets to C2 philosophy are the necessity of the subordinate commanders to execute operations independently but in accordance with a thorough understanding of the commander's intent, and command by negation or mission command. Once missions and functions are assigned, the subordinate commander is expected to take required actions without delay, keeping the superior commander informed of the situation. The superior commander retains the authority to negate any particular action. JMO tend to be decentralized. As such, mission command is the preferred method of C2.

b. Mission command is the conduct of military operations through decentralized execution based upon mission-type orders. Success demands that subordinate leaders at all echelons exercise disciplined initiative and act aggressively and independently to accomplish the mission. Essential to mission command is the thorough understanding of the commander's intent at every level of command. Commanders issue mission-type orders focused on the purpose of the operation rather than on the details of how to perform assigned tasks. They delegate decision-making authority to subordinates wherever possible, to minimize detailed control and empower subordinates to take initiative and make decisions based on understanding of the commander's intent rather than on constant communications.

When JMO are decentralized and reliant on mission command, coordination and planning considerations should include the procedures, measures, and resources (including time) required to implement those plans. The JFMCC and staff should anticipate requirements for joint support, prioritization of operations or force elements, and extensive coordination with other affected components.

3. Maritime Capabilities and Missions

There are five core capabilities of US naval forces: forward presence, deterrence, sea control, maritime power projection, and maritime security. Additional naval capabilities include foreign humanitarian assistance (FHA), strategic sealift, seabasing, and homeland security support.

a. **Forward Presence.** Forward presence activities demonstrate US commitment to the region, lend credibility to US alliances, enhance regional stability, and provide a crisis response capability while promoting US influence, freedom of navigation, and access. Joint force presence often keeps unstable situations from escalating into larger conflicts. The sustained presence of capable forces is a visible sign of US commitment to allies and adversaries alike. However, if forward presence fails to deter an adversary, those forces must be agile enough to transition rapidly to combat operations. Given their location and knowledge of the region, forward presence forces could be the first that a combatant commander (CCDR) commits when responding to a crisis. The maritime forces forward operating posture serves other key functions: it provides familiarity with the operational environment (OE) and contributes to an understanding of the capabilities, culture, and behavior patterns of regional actors. Forward presence supports security assistance, security cooperation activities, nation assistance, foreign internal defense programs, and provides credible combat power (deterrence and show of force). Through seabasing and the use of the non-sovereign, maneuver space that is the sea, the US possesses a broad range of options, generally unfettered by the requirement to obtain host nation (HN) permissions and access.

b. **Deterrence.** Maritime deterrent capabilities include sea-based nuclear weapons, forward posturing of conventional combat power in key regions, and the ability to surge forces tailored to meet emerging crises and defend the US homeland. The ocean provides maneuver space that enhances nuclear deterrent effects by making it infeasible for an adversary to succeed in neutralizing US nuclear capability through a preemptive attack and impractical to possess an effective defense against a second strike.

c. **Sea Control**

(1) Sea control operations are those operations designed to secure use of the maritime domain by one's own forces and to prevent its use by the enemy. Sea control is the essence of seapower and is a necessary ingredient in the successful accomplishment of all naval missions. Sea control and power projection complement one another. Sea control allows naval forces to close within striking distance to remove landward threats to access, which in turn enhances freedom of action at sea. Freedom of action at sea enables the projection of forces ashore. Sea control operations are the employment of naval forces, supported by land, air, space, cyberspace, and other forces as appropriate, in order to achieve

military objectives in vital sea areas. Such operations include destruction of enemy naval forces, suppression of enemy sea commerce, protection of vital sea lanes, and establishment of local military superiority in areas of naval operations. The vastness of the world's oceans makes it impossible for even a preeminent naval power to achieve global maritime superiority. Thus, achieving local or regional maritime superiority may be desired by the JFC for a limited duration in order to accomplish specific objectives. Sea control requires capabilities in all aspects of the maritime domain, space, and cyberspace. It is therefore a joint, vice purely naval, challenge.

(2) JMO occur in blue-, green-, and brown-water environments, each with its own challenges. Operations in blue water (high seas and open oceans) require forces capable of remaining on station for extended periods largely unrestricted by sea state and with logistics capability to sustain these forces indefinitely. Operations in green water (coastal waters, ports, and harbors) stretching seaward, require ships, amphibious ships and landing craft, and patrol craft with the stability and agility to operate effectively in surf, in shallows, and the near-shore areas of the littorals. Brown-water (navigable rivers, lakes, bays, and their estuaries) operations involve shallows and congested areas that constrain maneuver but do not subject maritime forces to extreme surf conditions.

d. **Maritime Power Projection.** The US possesses the ability to project significant power from the sea. Power projection in and from the maritime domain includes a broad spectrum of offensive military operations to destroy enemy forces, their logistic support, or to prevent enemy forces from approaching within enemy weapons range of friendly forces. Credible power projection supports deterrence objectives and activities. Power projection may be accomplished by an amphibious raid or assault, attack of targets ashore (e.g., strike operations, close air support [CAS], naval surface fire support [NSFS], BMD), sea-control operations, operations conducted from a seabase or combinations of these.

e. **Maritime Security.** The safety and economic security of the US depends in substantial part upon the secure use of the world's oceans. Maritime security operations (MSO) are conducted to assist in establishing the conditions for security and protection of sovereignty in the maritime domain. MSO are those operations to protect maritime sovereignty and resources and to counter maritime-related terrorism, weapons proliferation, transnational crime, piracy, environmental destruction, and illegal seaborne immigration. Terrorists, pirates, and transnational criminals use legitimate maritime traffic to mask their illicit activities, threatening safety and security. Identifying, tracking, and neutralizing these threats and illicit activities is essential to protecting national security and the global economy. Additional tasks include assisting mariners in distress, participating in security cooperation operations with allies and partners, sharing situational awareness, and conducting maritime interception and law enforcement operations (LEO). MSO involves close coordination among governments, the private sector, international organizations, and nongovernmental organizations (NGOs).

For more information on MSO, see Joint Publication (JP) 3-07.4, Counterdrug Operations, *and Naval Warfare Publication (NWP) 3-10,* Maritime Expeditionary Security Operations (MESO).

f. **Strategic Sealift.** Successful response to regional contingencies depends on sufficient strategic mobility assets in order to deploy combat forces rapidly and sustain them in an operational area as long as necessary to meet US military objectives. Strategic sealift delivers the heavy combat units and their support equipment as well as the vital sustainment for deployed forces. The application of strategic sealift divides into three broad categories: pre-positioning, surge shipping during initial mobilization, and sustainment shipping. The geographic combatant commander's (GCCs) joint deployment and distribution operations center (JDDOC) is the primary interface with United States Transportation Command. If established, the joint movement center will work closely with the JDDOC to execute theater movement control and prioritization. A related mission, in combination with maritime security, is the protection of other non-strategic sealift merchant shipping. During periods of crisis, conflict, national emergency or war the NCAGS is the principal US resource to facilitate the efficient management and safe passage of merchant ships that are not performing strategic sealift functions. The NCAGS' shipping coordination centers (SCCs) are regionally focused to support the JFC though the JFMCC in improving maritime domain awareness (MDA) as it relates to merchant shipping (other than strategic sealift). SCCs are responsible for maintaining and refining commercial shipping information within the common operational picture (COP).

g. **Seabasing.** Seabasing is the deployment, assembly, command, projection, sustainment, reconstitution, and re-employment of joint combat power from the sea without the reliance on land bases. It allows operational maneuver, and assured access to the joint force, while significantly reducing the footprint ashore, and minimizing permissions required to operate from HNs. Seabasing allows certain support functions to remain aboard ship until specifically required. With operational and logistics capabilities at sea, the sea base is able to operate from international waters, while providing support to the joint force on land. Seabasing improves freedom of action, achieved through sea control, and increases the maneuver options for joint forces by reducing the need to protect elements such as C2 and logistic nodes.

h. **Homeland Security Support.** Maritime forces may also support USCG in achieving its homeland security missions. USCG's competencies and resources in support of the *National Military Strategy* and other national-level defense and security strategies include maritime interception and interdiction operations; marine environmental protection; port waterways and coastal security; coastal sea control; rotary wing air intercept; combating terrorism; and maritime operational threat response (MOTR) plan support.

4. Interrelationship with Other Joint Operations

a. JMO are operations performed with maritime forces and other forces assigned, attached, or made available, in support of the JFC's operation or campaign objectives, or in support of other components of the joint force. The JFC may designate a JFMCC to C2 a JMO. As a functional component commander, the JFMCC has authority over assigned and attached forces and forces made available for tasking.

b. The degree of integration and coordination between joint force component commanders varies depending on the situation. For some JMO, the JFMCC will likely operate without the support of other Service component forces (e.g., submarine operations in blue water) whereas for others there may be detailed integration between components (e.g., attack of enemy submarines in port or their supporting critical infrastructures ashore). In other cases, tactical control (TACON) of maritime forces is delegated to other joint force components (e.g., CAS and strategic attack). For sea control operations, another joint force component may delegate TACON of forces to the JFMCC (e.g., maritime air support [MAS] during the conduct of surface warfare (SUW) operations). In certain cases, specification of operational control (OPCON) or TACON of forces may not be practical. In these cases, the JFC should establish a support command relationship, as required. All major operations generally necessitate some degree of maritime support to deploy, sustain, withdraw, and redeploy forces.

c. A JFC should consider the advantages of establishing a sea base to stage or support joint operations. Joint seabasing reduces the footprint ashore and allows support and sustainment to be landed in sufficient quantities, as required, without necessarily placing it all in a vulnerable and essentially immobile location. Seabasing reduces the possible negative impact on limited infrastructure ashore and facilitates the protection of logistics support. Additional information related to establishing, maintaining, and operating from a seabase can be found in NWP 3-62M, *Seabasing.*

5. Maritime Domain

JFCs, JFMCCs, and those supporting JMO require an understanding of the maritime domain and the capabilities of those maritime forces executing or supporting the joint mission.

a. Description and Characteristics

(1) The maritime domain is the oceans, seas, bays, estuaries, islands, coastal areas, and the airspace above these, including the littorals. Per JP 2-01.3, *Joint Intelligence Preparation of the Operational Environment,* the littoral comprises two segments of the OE. First, "seaward: the area from the shore to the open ocean, which must be controlled to support operations ashore." Second, "landward: the area inland from the shore that can be supported and defended directly from the sea."

(2) The maritime domain also has unique economic, diplomatic, military, and legal aspects (see Figure I-1). US naval forces operate in deep waters of the open ocean and other maritime environments including coastal areas, rivers, estuaries, and landward portions of the littorals, including associated airspace. In many regions of the world, rivers mark and define international borders and facilitate intracontinental trade. Ensuring access and securing these waterways are often priorities of state governments seeking to maintain stability and sovereignty. There are several thousand straits connecting the world's oceans, but only about 200 are the most vulnerable seaway chokepoints and lines of communications (LOCs). Adversaries may attempt to control the use of an internationally recognized strait by restricting access or disrupting passage of friendly naval forces or merchant shipping. In the event of regional conflict, small coastal navies operating in the proximity of these straits can present a serious challenge to the operations of naval forces and merchant shipping.

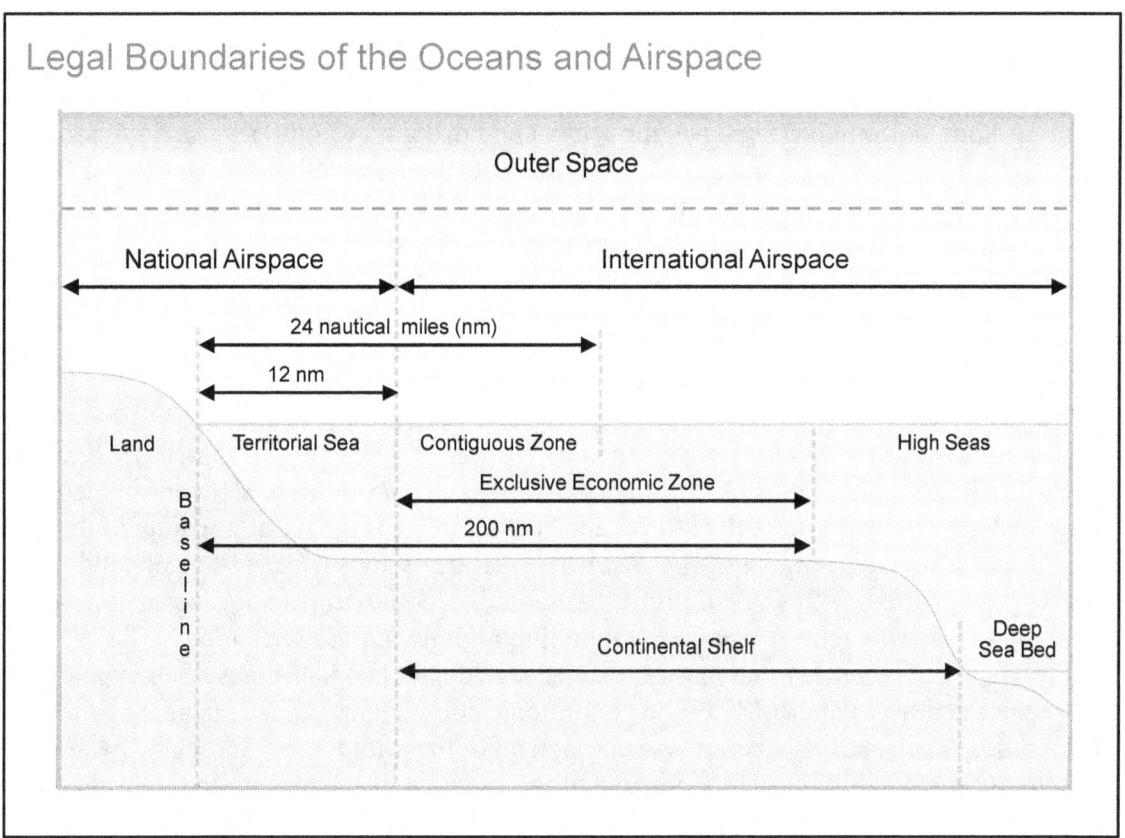

Figure I-1. Legal Boundaries of the Oceans and Airspace

Diplomatic and political issues related to the maritime domain have increased as many nations have tried to extend their claims over offshore resources. These claims have led to disputes over the exact extent of maritime borders and exclusive economic zones (EEZs). This is highlighted in diplomatic and legal tension over some archipelagic waters and international straits. Naval forces may face constraints and restrictions when operating in territorial seas, contiguous zones, EEZs, and continental shelves claimed by coastal states.

(3) The US currently recognizes approximately 150 navies in the world. Navies of the world may be categorized within a broad spectrum of demonstrated capabilities and political mandates. Naval capability as demonstrated projection of power may be viewed as global, regional, territorial, and coastal/self defense force. The great majority of the world's navies are small and capable of operating only in their respective littoral waters or constabulary navies. Only a few navies are capable of sustained employment far from their countries shores. However, whether or not their navies are capable of global power projection, most maritime nations also maintain air forces capable of conducting operations over the adjacent maritime domain. This air capability should be considered while planning operations in the maritime domain. Likewise, the multi-mission capabilities of modern naval platforms and their ability to project power should be a planning consideration. Ships and aircraft, regardless of source (adversary, neutral, friendly) are constantly in motion, thereby presenting additional challenges for the operational commander to gain and maintain situational awareness.

(4) The physical properties of the land-sea and air-sea interfaces, some unique undersea properties, and the sheer vastness of the maritime domain, render the sea largely opaque to many sensors. It provides a hiding place for smuggling operations, submarines firing missiles, and conducting naval movement and maneuver. While surface ships can be detected by a wide range of sensors including satellite or air surveillance, it is often difficult to identify specific vessels as targets with sufficient certainty to engage them, especially if they are not radiating distinctive electromagnetic and acoustic signatures. Additionally, weather conditions can change rapidly, and selected characteristics such as wave height and sea spray may impact visibility and radar or sensor effectiveness of platforms and munitions.

b. **Maritime Domain Awareness**

(1) National Security Presidential Directive (NSPD)-41/Homeland Security Presidential Directive (HSPD)-13, *Maritime Security Policy,* directs a coordinated and integrated government-wide effort to enhance the security of the maritime domain through the *National Strategy for Maritime Security.* MDA is the effective understanding of anything associated with the maritime domain that could impact the security, safety, economy or environment of a nation. Obtaining and maintaining accurate MDA is a key enabler of an active and layered maritime defense in depth, and facilitates more expeditious and precise actions by the JFMCC and subordinate commanders. Some degree of MDA is also required to effectively operate as a component of the joint force. Achieving awareness of the maritime domain is challenging due to the vastness of the oceans and seas, the large volume of maritime commerce, sensor limitations, the great length of shorelines, and size of port areas which provide both concealment and numerous access points to the land. MDA requires integrating all-source intelligence, law enforcement information, open-source data, and information from public and private sectors, both nationally and internationally.

(2) The primary method for information sharing, gaining situational awareness, and supporting collaborative planning in the maritime domain is through development and maintenance of a global maritime COP. Networking maritime regions and resources into a COP can present useful data in a form that supports a wide range of planning, decision, execution, and assessment requirements. This data can also support GCC requirements to achieve an area of responsibility (AOR)-wide, single integrated COP. The maritime data can range from a global "snapshot" to the detailed information required by the JFMCC and subordinate commanders within their specific operational area.

c. **Movement and Maneuver**

(1) The JFMCC directs subordinate commanders in the execution of force-level operational tasks, advises the JFC of its movement, and coordinates with other components and interorganizational entities supporting or affected by JMO.

(2) Operational movement and maneuver includes moving or deploying forces for operational advantage into an operational area and conducting maneuver for offensive or defensive purposes. It includes providing freedom of movement and maneuver to friendly forces and controlling the OE on land, on and under the sea, in the air, or in space where it provides an operational advantage.

(3) Often key attributes of the JFMCCs concept of operations (CONOPS), movement and maneuver in the maritime domain can help gain the element of surprise and provide a significant advantage over adversaries, while allowing the commander to rapidly concentrate forces when necessary.

(4) Movement and maneuver using maritime forces are integral to joint operations. During maritime operations, commanders use information and initiative to apply decisive force and dominate specific regions and dimensions of the environment at the chosen time and place. Maintaining awareness in the transition from the open ocean to littoral areas is key to the continuing conduct of maneuver on and from the sea. Whether done at, under, or from the sea, maneuver can provide significant advantages in the application of maritime power projection in support of joint force operations. Some of the movement details and schemes of maneuver are articulated in JFC and JFMCC tasking documents which include timing, sequencing, method, and location of entry into the assigned area of operations (AO).

Intentionally Blank

CHAPTER II
ORGANIZING FOR JOINT MARITIME OPERATIONS

"The Navy, Marine Corps, and Coast Guard are the principal organizations that conduct military operations over, on, under, and adjacent to the sea, overlying airspace, surface, subsurface, and the ocean bottom, as well as the shoreline infrastructures that affect maritime operations."

Naval Operating Concept 2010

1. General Organizational Options

a. JFCs organize staffs and forces to accomplish the mission based on their vision and CONOPS. Organizing the maritime force and staffs should take into account the nature of today's complex global environment, technological advances in communications, intelligence, surveillance, and reconnaissance (ISR) systems, improved weapons capabilities, and how multinational forces organize, train, equip, and conduct operations. Equally important in determining how a JFC organizes joint forces are an adversary's nature, capabilities, and the OE (e.g., geography, accessibility, climate, and infrastructure).

b. Naval command relationships are based on a philosophy of mission command involving centralized guidance, collaborative planning, and decentralized control and execution. With a long-standing practice of using mission-type orders, naval C2 practices are intended to achieve relative advantage through organizational ability to rapidly observe, orient, decide, and act. Mission-type orders enable continued operations in environments where communications are restricted, compromised or denied, allowing subordinates to exercise disciplined initiative (consistent with the higher commander's intent) and act aggressively and independently to accomplish the mission.

c. Since the JFC normally designates a Service component commander to also serve as a functional component commander, the dual-designated Service/functional component commander will normally exercise OPCON as a Service component commander over their own Service forces, and TACON as a functional component commander over other Services forces made available for tasking. Navy multi-mission ships are rarely made available for tasking outside the maritime component, because their multi-mission capabilities will require them to fulfill JFMCC operational requirements.

d. Forward deployed maritime force packages are normally comprised of units that train together prior to deploying. These tailored force packages may include carrier strike groups (CSGs) and amphibious ready groups (ARGs) with an embarked Marine expeditionary unit (MEU). Force packages can be scaled up by adding ships and capabilities, or scaled down into smaller surface action groups, individual ships, or special purpose forces designed to conduct numerous types of military operations.

e. ARGs with embarked MEUs (ARG/MEU) are postured forward in key regions to support security cooperation and deterrence, or provide immediate response to crisis and contingencies. The ARG/MEU is organized, trained, and equipped to operate as a mutually supporting force. However, it also has the ability to conduct simultaneous, geographically dispersed operations; albeit with some reduced capability.

f. The JFMCC's staff planning process is consistent with the joint operation planning process (JOPP) as outlined in JP 5-0, *Joint Operation Planning*. The JFMCC's staff uses a synchronization process similar to a JFC's staff to ensure coordination between subordinates. All levels of command have processes for analysis and assessment during execution. Collaboration is critical to the synchronization of planning, execution, and assessment processes and enables multiple echelons to work efficiently and effectively together. Creating timely mechanisms for systematic assessment and decision-making enable the entire force to rapidly adapt and leverage opportunities in complex dynamic environments.

> A baseline carrier strike group consists of an aircraft carrier, carrier air wing, up to five surface combatants (three of which are normally land attack cruise missile capable), a fleet oiler, and a direct support submarine. The baseline amphibious ready group with embarked Marine expeditionary unit (ARG/MEU) includes an amphibious assault ship (LHA [amphibious assault ship, general purpose] or LHD [amphibious assault ship, multipurpose]), a LPD (amphibious transport dock), and a LSD (dock landing ship) while the MEU includes a command element, ground combat element, aviation combat element, and logistics combat element.

g. The JFC establishes subordinate commands, assigns responsibilities, establishes appropriate command relationships, provides coordinating instructions to optimize the capabilities of each subordinate, and gains synergistic effects for the joint force as a whole. The JFC may designate a JFMCC to facilitate unity of effort, focus, and synchronize efforts while providing subordinate commanders flexibility and opportunity in exercising initiative and maintaining the joint forces' operational tempo.

(1) Most often, joint forces are organized with a combination of Service and functional component commands and subordinate task forces (TFs) with operational responsibilities (see Figure II-1). The JFC normally designates the forces and maritime assets that will be made available for tasking by the JFMCC, and delegates the appropriate command authority the JFMCC will exercise over assigned and attached forces and maritime assets made available for tasking. Generally, these forces and maritime assets include navies, marines/naval infantries, special operations forces (SOF), coast guards and similar border patrol and revenue services, nonmilitary shipping managed by the government, civil merchant marines, army/ground forces (normally when embarked), and air and air defense forces. Establishment of a JFMCC must not affect the command relationships between Service component commanders and the JFC.

(2) In cases where the JFC does not designate a JFMCC, the JFC may elect to directly task maritime forces. Typically, this would occur when an operation is of limited duration, scope, or complexity. If this option is exercised, the JFC's staff assists in planning

Typical Joint Force Maritime Component Commander Responsibilities

- Develop a joint maritime operations plan to best support joint force objectives.

- Provide centralized direction for the allocation and tasking of forces/capabilities made available.

- Request forces of other component commanders when necessary for the accomplishment of the maritime mission.

- Make maritime apportionment recommendations to the joint force commander (JFC).

- Provide maritime forces to other component commanders in accordance with JFC maritime apportionment decisions.

- Control the operational level synchronization and execution of joint maritime operations, as specified by the JFC, to include adjusting targets and tasks for available joint capabilities/forces. The JFC and affected component commanders will be notified, as appropriate, if the joint force maritime component commander (JFMCC) changes the planned joint maritime operations during execution.

- Act as supported commander within the assigned area of operations (AO).

- Assign and coordinate target priorities within the assigned AO by synchronizing and integrating maneuver, mobility and movement, fires, and interdiction. The JFMCC nominates targets located within the maritime AO to the joint targeting process that may potentially require action by another component commander's assigned forces.

- Evaluate results of maritime operations and forward assessments to the JFC in support of the overall effort.

- Support JFC information operations with assigned assets, when directed.

- Function as a supported and supporting commander, as directed by the JFC.

- Perform other functions, as directed by the JFC.

- Establish a personnel recovery coordination cell to account for and report the status of isolated personnel and to coordinate and control maritime component personnel recovery events; and, if directed by the JFC, establish a separate joint personnel recovery center for the same purpose in support of a joint recovery event.

- Coordinate the planning and execution of joint maritime operations with the other components and supporting agencies.

- Integrate the JFMCC's communications systems and resources into the theaters networked communications system architecture, or common operational picture, and synchronize JFMCC's critical voice and data requirements. Ensure these communications systems requirements, coordination issues, and capabilities are integrated in the joint planning and execution process.

Figure II-1. Typical Joint Force Maritime Component Commander Responsibilities

and coordinating maritime operations for JFC approval. The JFC may elect to centralize selected functions (planning, coordinating, and tasking) within the staff to provide direction, control, and coordination of the joint force.

2. Component Employment Considerations

a. **Weighing Options.** When the JFC designates a JFMCC, the JFMCC's authority and responsibility are also defined by the JFC. The following are some considerations for establishing JFMCC authorities, responsibilities, and timing:

(1) **Planning.** There is a need for detailed, coordinated, concurrent, and parallel planning. While JFMCC integrated planning is focused primarily on employment, the JFMCC may also be tasked to integrate planning of multi-Service maritime forces for deployment, transition, redeployment, or reconstitution at a level subordinate to that of the JFC.

(2) **Duration.** The projected length of an operation should be of sufficient duration to warrant the establishment of a JFMCC. The decision to establish a JFMCC should also consider the time required for additional personnel and staff sourcing and training, the establishment of C2 alterations, and necessary communications system support architecture upgrades.

(3) **Maritime Perspective.** The JFC desires the focused maritime expertise of a JFMCC and staff to enhance the detailed planning, coordination, and execution of JMO.

(4) **JFC Span of Control.** When task complexities, JFC staff organizational or resource limitations and environmental intricacies limit the JFC's effective span of control, empowering functional components can provide the flexibility and initiative required for success.

(5) **Timing.** To permit the JFMCC to fully participate in planning and to maximize unity of effort, the decision to establish and designate a JFMCC should occur well before the concept development phase of the operation or campaign plan. JFMCC representatives should be identified and involved in planning as early as possible.

b. **Service Component Command**

(1) All joint forces include Service component commands to address administrative and logistic support for Service forces. The JFC may choose to conduct operations through a Service component commander or, at lower echelons, a Service force commander. This most often happens when there are no other Service or multinational maritime capabilities provided as part of the joint force; and the scope of operations along with the need for stability, continuity, economy, and ease of long-range planning dictate organizational integrity of Service forces for conducting operations.

(2) An Navy component commander (NCC) assigned to a CCDR consists of the NCC and the Navy forces (NAVFOR) that have been assigned to that CCDR. A Marine component command assigned to a CCDR consists of the Marine component commander and the Marine forces that have been assigned to that CCDR. When a Service command is designated as the naval or maritime component to multiple CCDRs, the commander and only those specific forces assigned to that particular CCDR are under the combatant command (CCMD) (command authority) of that particular CCDR.

(3) In instances where an NCC is not assigned, NAVFOR may be attached as a Navy Service component through the request for forces process. When attached, this Navy Service component includes NAVFOR, a designated commander, and appropriate command element.

c. **Selecting a Commander.** The JFC establishing a functional component command has the authority to designate its commander. Normally, the Service component commander with the preponderance of forces to be tasked, and the ability to C2 those forces will be designated as the functional component commander; however, the JFC will always consider the mission, nature and duration of the operation, force capabilities, and the C2 capabilities in selecting a commander. In the maritime domain, especially the littorals, circumstances may dictate that a Marine Corps or Coast Guard officer be designated the JFMCC.

3. Command Relationships and Responsibilities

a. **Command Relationships Applicable to the Joint Force Maritime Component Commander**

(1) JFMCC responsibilities for integrating JMO include, but are not limited to, planning, coordination, allocation, and tasking of JMO based on the JFC's CONOPS and apportionment decisions. Specific responsibilities that normally are assigned to the JFMCC are included in Figure II-1.

(2) The JFC establishes the authority and command relationships of the JFMCC. The JFMCC normally exercises OPCON over assigned forces and OPCON or TACON over attached forces. Additionally, the JFMCC may exercise TACON over other military capabilities and forces made available for tasking. Regardless of organizational and command arrangements within joint commands, Service component commanders are responsible for certain Service-specific functions and other matters affecting their forces: internal administration, training, logistics and Service-unique intelligence operations. The JFMCC should be aware of all such Service-specific responsibilities.

b. **Area of Operations**

(1) When a JFMCC is established, the JFC will normally designate an AO. JFCs establish maritime AOs to decentralize execution of maritime component operations, allow rapid maneuver, and provide the ability to fight at extended ranges. The size, shape, and positioning of land or maritime AOs will be based on the JFC's CONOPS and the land or maritime commander's requirements to accomplish their missions and protect their forces. The AO can be dynamic and evolve as the operation or campaign matures. It should be of sufficient size to allow for movement, maneuver, and employment of weapons systems, effective utilization of warfighting capabilities, and provide operational depth for logistics and force protection (FP). Within the AO, the JFMCC establishes subordinate maneuver space that allows for independent yet supporting operations of subordinate elements while enabling the synchronized and effective employment of forces across all components. The AO may not encompass the entire littoral area; however, it should be large enough for the

JFMCC to accomplish the mission and protect the maritime force. The AO may include air, land, and sea.

(2) When the JFC designates a maritime AO, the JFMCC is the supported commander within the AO. As supported commander, the JFMCC integrates and synchronizes maneuver, fires, and interdiction. To facilitate integration and synchronization, JFMCC has the authority to designate target priority, effects, and timing of fires within the AO.

(3) In coordination with the JFMCC, other commanders designated by the JFC to execute theater- or joint operations area (JOA)- wide functions have the latitude to plan and execute these JFC- prioritized operations within the maritime AO. Commanders executing such a mission must coordinate the operation to avoid adverse effects. If those operations would have adverse impact within the maritime AO, the commander assigned to execute the JOA-wide functions shall readjust the plan, resolve the issue with the JFMCC, or consult with the JFC for resolution.

c. **Joint Force Maritime Component Commander Functions.** The JFMCC executes the operational functions discussed below and can functionally organize to accomplish missions.

(1) **Command and Control.** The JFMCC commands assigned and attached forces, prepares supporting plans to the JFC operation plans (OPLANs), and executes operations as directed by the JFC. Upon JFC approval of the JFMCC's CONOPS or scheme of maneuver, the JFMCC exercises specified authority and direction over forces in the accomplishment of the assigned mission. The JFMCC assigns tasks and operating areas, prioritizes and allocates resources, manages risk, and publishes operational and daily tasking orders for the execution of maritime operational activity. The JFMCC also maintains liaison with other components and the joint force headquarters (HQ) to provide JFMCC representation as required to provide timely coordination and achieve unity of effort.

For more information on the C2 function, see JP 3-0, Joint Operations.

(a) **Planning.** The JFMCC assists the JFC in planning, preparation of OPLANs, and associated estimates of the situation. JFMCCs planning responsibilities include:

1. Develop a maritime supporting plan to best support joint force CONOPS and objectives, as assigned.

2. Develop maritime courses of action (COAs) within the framework of the JFC-assigned objective or mission, the forces available, and the commanders intent.

3. Coordinate planning with higher, lower, adjacent, supporting, and multinational HQ.

4. Determine forces required and coordinate deployment planning in support of the selected COAs.

<u>5</u>. Coordinate the planning and execution of maneuver operations with other missions.

(b) The JFMCC makes recommendations to the JFC on the employment, support, coordination, and assessment of maritime forces. Such recommendations should include:

<u>1</u>. Maritime force structure requirements.

<u>2</u>. Integration and employment of multinational maritime forces.

<u>3</u>. Priorities of effort.

<u>4</u>. Operational limitations.

<u>5</u>. Intelligence collection priorities.

<u>6</u>. Space support.

<u>7</u>. Cyberspace operations.

<u>8</u>. Assessment of JMO to include measures of effectiveness (MOEs) and measures of performance (MOPs).

(c) **Coordination and Deconfliction.** Where and when appropriate, the JFMCC makes coordination and deconfliction recommendations to the JFC, to include airspace management, land-space management, waterspace management (WSM), fire support coordination measures, target priorities, electromagnetic spectrum management, cyberspace operations, interorganizational coordination, and liaison requirements.

(2) **Intelligence.** Understanding the OE is fundamental to joint operations. JFMCC input to provide the maritime perspective of the OE is crucial. Intelligence should be sufficiently detailed and timely to satisfy the commanders decision-making needs. The JFMCC provides a unique complement of sensors and sensor fusion capability to support joint requirements and advocates for the use of other component and national assets to provide optimum support to maritime operations. Sonar capabilities and the ability to relocate surveillance and reconnaissance assets may provide additional options to the JFC. Close coordination with other component commanders and the communications system directorate of a joint staff (J-6) early in joint planning is essential to aligning architectures with platform and sensor employment plans to optimize intelligence, surveillance, reconnaissance, and associated processing, exploitation, and dissemination systems throughout the joint force. The complexity of operating in the maritime domain require a baseline of organic ISR in addition to any joint forces and capabilities allocated to maintain MDA and to succeed in military operations. NCCs typically retain OPCON of organic ISR capabilities (manned and unmanned) to enable MDA and fully support the integrated employment of maritime capabilities.

For more information on the intelligence function, see JP 3-0, Joint Operations.

(3) **Movement and Maneuver.** The JFMCC is responsible for the movement and maneuver of assigned and attached forces. The JFMCC makes recommendations to the JFC regarding sealift and seabasing, the movement of supporting forces, and coordination of the movement or maneuver of other component forces through the maritime AO.

For more information on the movement and maneuver function, see JP 3-0, Joint Operations.

(4) **Fires.** The JFMCC is responsible for the planning and employment of operational fires within the assigned AO, both in terms of developing and integrating multidimensional attacks on the adversary's centers of gravity (COGs) and in terms of shaping the JFMCC's AO.

For more information on the fires function, see JP 3-0, Joint Operations.

(5) **Protection.** The protection function focuses on preserving the maritime forces' fighting potential in four primary ways: active defensive measures, passive defensive measures, the application of technology and procedures, and emergency management and response. As the mission requires, the protection function also extends to encompass protection of US civilians; the forces, systems, and civil infrastructure of friendly nations; and interorganizational partners. The JFMCC is responsible for all aspects of protection and maritime FP within the assigned AO. FP is part of each mission assigned to maritime forces and includes antiterrorism, physical security, and personal security. The GCC exercises TACON for FP of all Department of Defense (DOD) forces in the AOR and stipulates how the TACON for FP of NAVFOR is delegated. The delegation of TACON for FP is most commonly done along, but is not limited to, Service or functional component lines, or geographically determined sectors.

(6) **Sustainment.** Sustainment is the provision of logistics and personnel services necessary to maintain and prolong operations through mission accomplishment and redeployment of the force. The JFMCC makes recommendations concerning the distribution of material and services commensurate with priorities developed for JFMCC operations. A GCC may delegate responsibility for a common support capability to the JFMCC. The JFMCC will usually coordinate sustainment delivery for all forces operating from a sea base. For more guidance on the sustainment function, see JP 3-0, *Joint Operations,* and JP 4-0, *Joint Logistics.*

4. Organizing and Manning the Component Headquarters

a. The component HQ, organization and staffing, will differ depending upon the mission, environment, existing and potential adversaries, nature of the crisis (e.g., tsunami, cyclone, earthquake), time available, and desired end state. The JFMCC's staff is typically built from an existing Service component, numbered fleet, Marine air-ground task force (MAGTF), or subordinate Service force staff and then augmented as required. The commander should drive the formation process and consider the following factors:

(1) What are the specified and implied tasks?

(2) Does the staff need subject matter expertise augmentation to effectively perform the assigned mission?

(3) What is the desired and expected timeline for augmentees to arrive at the staff or to become available via reachback support from remote locations?

(4) What mitigating actions has the staff taken to fill short-term gaps until required expert augmentees arrive?

(5) If employing a forward command element (afloat or ashore), have specific requirements, responsibilities, and synchronization mechanisms for the split staff been designated?

(6) During split-staff operations, how will the commander's decisions and guidance be shared with the portion of the staff not physically located with the commander?

(7) Who on the staff is responsible for establishing and promulgating the battle rhythm (Figure II-2)?

b. In a maritime HQ two complementary methods of organizing people and processes exist. The first is the doctrinal J-code structure, which organizes people by the function they perform (i.e., intelligence, logistics). The second is a cross-functional approach that organizes the staff into boards, centers, cell, and working groups that manage specific processes or tasks that do not fit well under the J-code structure and require cross-functional participation, such as targeting, assessment, and information operations (IO). The fast pace of military operations and cross-talk needed to support an operational-level command has made the cross-functional approach the preferred manner of organization, while maintaining the doctrinal roles of the J-code structure. The maritime operations center (MOC) can be thought of as a loosely-bound network of staff entities overlaying the J-code structure. If a Navy component or numbered fleet commander is designated as the JFMCC, their existing staff or MOC will normally form the nucleus of the JFMCC staff or MOC. The formalized addition of this cross-functional network to the doctrinal J-code organizational structure is what constitutes the MOC. The MOC's focus is on operational tasks and activities (vice fleet management or support). It must be recognized, however, that when a commander establishes a MOC, the traditional staff code organization does not disappear. Indeed, the doctrinal J-code directorates are the foundation of the MOC. They supply the manpower, expertise, and facilities needed by the MOC to function. As a practical matter, the commander establishes and maintains only those boards, centers, cells, and working groups that enhance planning and decision making within the HQ. A fires cell, for example, is likely not required during a disaster relief operation. The commander establishes, modifies, and dissolves these functional entities as the needs of the command evolve.

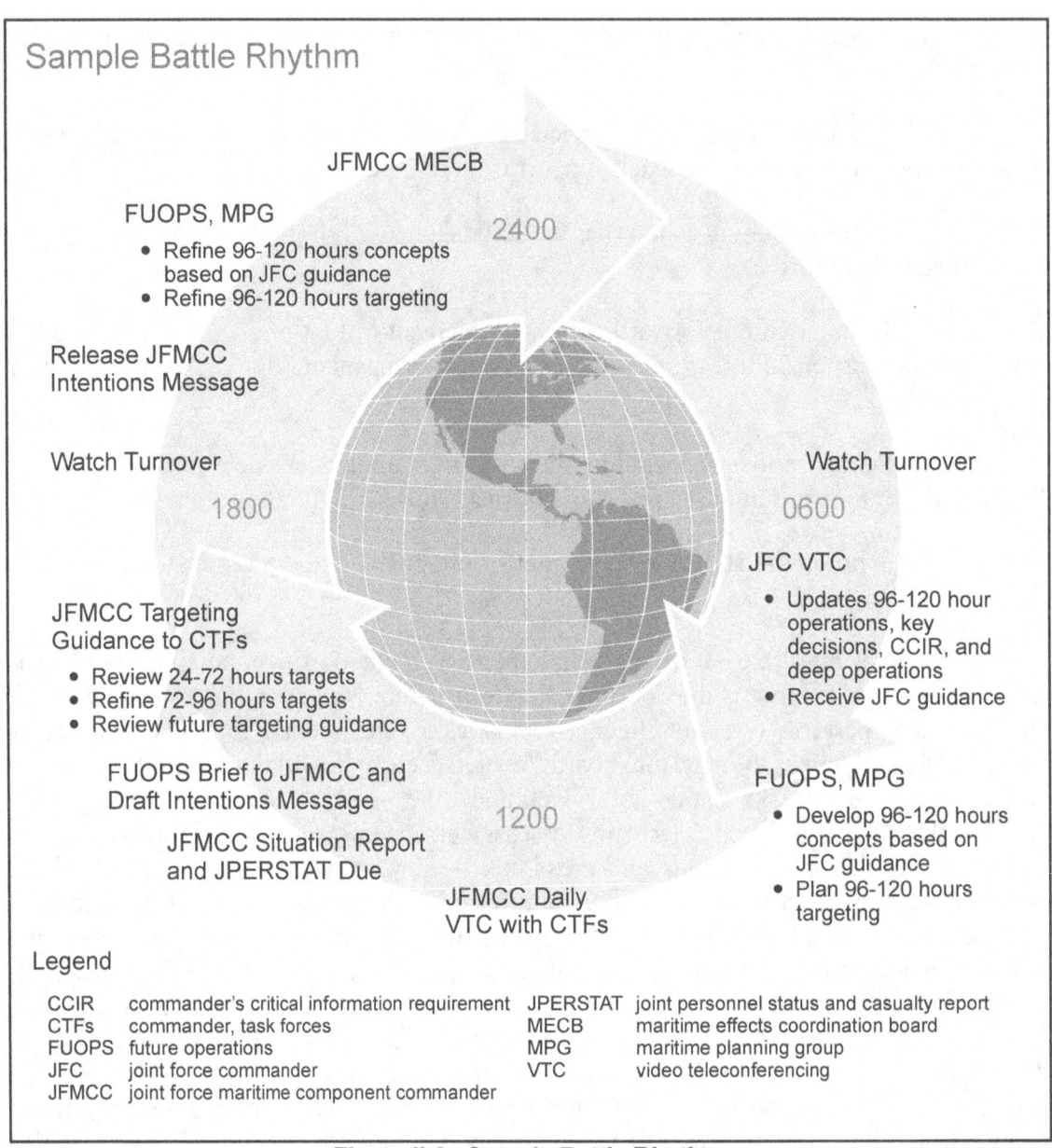

Figure II-2. Sample Battle Rhythm

The generic seven-minute drill (Figure II-3) is a tool to aid participants in understanding key information about the meeting and focus their participation in an efficient and productive manner. Key elements include the purpose, inputs, outputs, important members, and time-lines.

    c. MOCs provide an organizational framework through which maritime commanders may exercise operational-level C2.

    d. Liaison elements from and to other joint force and Service components are also considerations in composition and required infrastructure. Joint force command relationships, the nature of the mission, and standing Service agreements help determine

```
Generic Seven-Minute Drill Example

  UNCLASSIFIED
                    Boards, Centers, Cells, and Working Groups Validation
                                    "Seven Minute Drill"

    1.  Name of board or cell:  Descriptive and unique

    2.  Lead J code:  Who receives, compiles, and delivers information

    3.  When/where does it meet in battle rhythm?:  Allocation of resources (time and facilities),
        and any collaborative tool requirements

    4.  Purpose:  Brief description of the requirement

    5.  Inputs required from:  Staff sections and/or boards, centers, cells, and working groups
        required to provide products (once approved by chief of staff, these become specified
        tasks)

    6.  When? Suspense date-time group for inputs

    7.  Output/process/product:  Products and links to other staff organizations

    8.  Time of delivery:  When outputs will be available

    9.  Membership codes:  Who has to attend (task to staff to provide reps)

                                                                              UNCLASSIFIED
```

Figure II-3. Generic Seven-Minute Drill Example

liaison manning requirements. For more information on Navy MOCs, see Navy Tactics, Techniques, and Procedures (NTTP) 3-32.1, *Maritime Operations Center*.

5. Task Organization of Subordinate Forces

a. The JFMCC normally delegates the authority to plan and execute tactical missions to subordinate TF or task group commanders. This enables the JFMCC to focus attention on the operational level and empowers subordinate commanders to employ their forces to support the commander's intent. Individual platforms are assigned or attached to these subordinate TFs. Each TF is assigned a commander, and only the commander reports to the JFMCC. The commander, task force (CTF), may further subdivide the TF into task groups, units, and elements to exercise control at the tactical level. These subdivisions may be organized based on capabilities, missions, geography, or a hybrid of all three. Only a commander with OPCON or North Atlantic Treaty Organization (NATO) operational command can assign or attach units to subcomponents in the task organization structure.

b. The MAGTF is the Marine Corps' principal organizational construct for conducting missions across the range of military operations. MAGTFs provide CCDRs with scalable, versatile expeditionary force able to assure allies, deter potential adversaries, provide persistent US presence with little or no footprint ashore, and respond to broad range of contingency, crisis, and conflict situations. They are balanced combined arms force packages containing organic command, ground, aviation, and logistics elements. A single commander leads and coordinates this combined-arms team through all phases of deployment and employment. As the name indicates, MAGTFs are organized for the specific tasks at hand and specifically tailored by mission for rapid deployment by air and/or sea.

6. Navy Composite Warfare Doctrine

a. The officer in tactical command (OTC) is the senior officer present eligible to assume command, or the officer to whom the senior officer has delegated tactical command. The OTC is responsible for the tactical force deployment and action. The commander of a task organization is its OTC when the organization is operating independently. When task organizations at the same echelon operate with each other, the mutual agreement of the task organization commanders (often based on seniority) or the common superior define the command relationships that will exist between the commanders. The OTC can assign command functions to other commanders in the task component. This is the primary means by which commanders for each composite warfare functional areas are assigned. These warfare functional areas typically include SUW, air and missile defense (AMD), antisubmarine warfare (ASW), mine warfare (MIW), strike warfare (STW), IO, and others as required.

b. When warfare functions are assigned to subordinate commanders, it is assumed that the necessary authority for command, control, direction, and coordination required for the execution of that function is delegated with it. When multiple warfare functions (e.g., AMD, ASW, IO, and SUW) are assigned, the OTC also designates a composite warfare commander (CWC) to coordinate overall operations. The OTC may choose to function as the CWC. While acknowledged in joint doctrine, the OTC and CWC are Navy and NATO unique constructs. Joint community understanding of these C2 constructs is important when coordinating or working with maritime forces. The OTC controls CWC and subordinate warfare commander's actions through "command by negation". Allied maritime procedures and instructions use the term "command by veto" to mean the same thing. Command by negation acknowledges that in many aspects of often distributed and dispersed maritime warfare, it is necessary to pre-plan the actions of a force to an assessed threat and delegate some warfare functions to subordinate commanders. Once such functions are delegated, the subordinate commander is to take the required action without delay, always keeping the OTC informed of the situation. The CWC orchestrates operations to counter threats to the force, while the OTC retains close control of power projection and specific sea control operations. Each CWC focuses on its surveillance, classification, identification, and engagement areas (CIEAs) and vital areas. OTCs who are also CTFs have the concurrent responsibility for supporting the JFMCC's planning for maritime operations. Although assignment of various warfare commanders will allow control of different capabilities on a single platform by multiple commanders, only one commander may exercise TACON for the ship's movements and maneuver.

For additional information on composite warfare doctrine, see Chapter IV, "Command and Control and Other Operational-Level Consideration for Specific Maritime Operation;" NWP 3-56, Composite Warfare Doctrine; and Allied Tactical Publication (ATP)-1, Allied Maritime Tactical Instructions and Procedures.

7. Multinational Considerations

Command authority for a multinational force commander (MNFC) is normally negotiated between the participating nations and can vary from nation to nation. Command authority could range from OPCON, to TACON, to designated support relationships, to coordinating authority. The US, particularly the US Navy, frequently operates as an element of a NATO force and routinely uses NATO doctrine, tactics, techniques, and procedures (ratified by the US via standardization agreements [STANAGs]) to guide those operations.

For overarching doctrine on multinational operations, see JP 3-16, Multinational Operations. *For additional information on NATO maritime operations, see Allied Joint Publication (AJP) 3.1,* Allied Joint Maritime Operations.

8. Support to a Joint Force Air Component Commander Afloat

In operations where no shore-based air operations center (AOC) can initially be accommodated, the preponderance of capability to plan, task, and control joint air operations may be located afloat. This is most likely during the initial stages of forcible entry operations, cases where the US desires to limit the presence of forces ashore, or prior to the arrival of a shore-based AOC. Ideally, these operations will be of limited scope and/or short duration, as the ships capable of supporting these operations have limited communications infrastructure, workspace, berthing, and other facilities to host AOC and liaison officer (LNO) personnel.

Intentionally Blank

CHAPTER III
PLANNING JOINT MARITIME OPERATIONS

"A 19th-century sailor would be bewildered by a modern warship, but regardless of the appearance of ships, there is one element, the most important of all, that remains unchanged - the man himself. Human nature in all the changing years has altered but little. It is the human element in warfare which may, if understood by the commander, prove to be the only way of converting an impossibility into a successful reality. With trained men and proper materials, the commander's task is reduced to the preparation of good plans."

War Instructions, US Navy, 1944

1. Maritime Planning Processes and Products

a. Planning for the employment of military forces is an inherent responsibility of command. Joint planning integrates military actions with those of other instruments of national power and our multinational partners in time, space, and purpose to achieve a specified end state. Planning begins with the end state in mind, providing a unifying purpose around which actions and resources are focused. Military planning is a comprehensive process that enables commanders and staffs at all levels and in all services to make informed decisions, solve complex problems, and ultimately accomplish assigned missions. The JFMCC's operational-level planning simultaneously supports the strategic and operational requirements of the JFC and also frames the tactical-level requirements of subordinate commanders. The JFMCC's planning is driven by the JFC's guidance and intent, supports JFC staff planning efforts, and should be closely coordinated with component planning. In conducting joint operation planning, commanders and staff blend operational art, operational design, and the JOPP in complementary fashion as part of the overall process that produces the eventual plan or order that drives the joint operation. JOPP is an orderly, analytical process that consists of a set of logical steps to analyze a mission; develop, analyze, and compare alternative COAs; select the best COA; and produce a plan or order. Through JOPP, planners effectively translate the commanders planning guidance into a feasible COA and CONOPS by which the joint force can achieve its assigned mission and military end state. It involves simultaneous efforts to address near-term and far-term operations, and should be flexible enough to adjust to dynamic unforeseen situations and new taskings.

b. Most maritime platforms are multi-mission capable and are routinely multi-tasked to support different missions and warfare commanders. JFMCC, OTC, and CWCs and their staffs should be able to recognize and prioritize requirements, address conflicts and limitations, and integrate the various capabilities of assigned and attached forces and those made available for tasking. However, it is important to understand the implications of multi-mission tasking (e.g., ASW, STW, CAS, MAS, sea control) on individual platforms and personnel. Factoring these implications into decision making, especially regarding command relationships and employment, is paramount. Specific capabilities of a single multi-mission ship, or other maritime force, may be in direct support of one unit or warfare commander, while other capabilities inherent to that same platform are in general support of another. Another complication is that this often diverse tasking can change significantly and rapidly, as events in this complex environment unfold. The JFMCC manages these shifts in tasking and delineates how to provide this varied simultaneous support to sometimes geographically separated forces. The JFMCC management mechanism is normally via operation orders (OPORDs), fragmentary orders, operation general matter, and operation tasks (OPTASKs). This guidance and direction are normally updated daily, but may be modified more frequently (i.e., hourly). These directives should incorporate the JFC's intent, support approved subordinate CONOPS, consider requests prompted by the dynamics of the OE, work within the required operations tempo, and frame the daily operational planning conducted by the JFMCC's staff and assigned forces.

c. The maritime planning process assists commanders and their staffs in analyzing the OE and distilling information in order to provide the commander a coherent framework to support decisions. The process, which parallels the JOPP, is thorough and helps apply clarity, sound judgment, logic, and professional expertise. It provides commanders and their staffs a means to organize planning activities, transmit plans to tactical forces, and share a critical common understanding of the mission. Interaction among various planning steps allows a concurrent, coordinated effort and the flexibility required to make efficient use of available time. It also facilitates continuous information sharing.

2. Integration with Joint Operation Planning Process

JFMCCs and their staffs not only contribute to the JFC's planning efforts but should also contribute to the development of other joint force components' supporting plans and OPORDs. Therefore, maritime staffs should be well versed in the JOPP; the Chairman of the Joint Chiefs of Staff Manual (CJCSM) 3122 Series, *Joint Operation Planning and Execution System;* CJCSM 3130 Series, *Adaptive Planning and Execution,* JP 3-0, *Joint Operations;* JP 5-0, *Joint Operation Planning;* approved joint terminology; and the amphibious planning process contained in JP 3-02, *Amphibious Operations.* Multinational operations are the norm in the maritime domain, and multinational procedures (e.g., NATO STANAGs and ratified AJPs) may impact the maritime component's battle rhythm and processes more so than other joint force components. Therefore, maritime staffs may need to refer to NATO publications, such as AJP-3.1, *Allied Joint Maritime Operations,* AJP-3.3.3, *Air Maritime Co-ordination,* Maritime Tactical Publication-01, *Multinational Maritime Tactical Instructions and Procedures,* and Maritime Procedural Publication-01, *Multinational Maritime Voice Reporting Procedures.*

3. Organizing the Operational Area

a. Commanders and their staffs should assess friendly factors of space, time, forces, and degree of risk tolerance individually and then balance them in combination against the ultimate or intermediate objective. The balancing of operational factors versus objective in a major operation is determined by the framework of a campaign. Any serious disconnect or mismatch between the ultimate or intermediate objective and the corresponding space-time-force factors might complicate and possibly endanger the success of the operation. If the imbalance cannot be resolved, then the objective should be changed and brought into harmony with the operational factors. This process is complicated and time consuming. It is more an art than a science. In practice, operational factors will rarely be completely, or even approximately, in harmony with one another or with the assigned objective.

b. In harmonizing friendly operational factors against the respective objective, all considerations, when possible, should start with the quantifiable factors of space and time (i.e., operational reach). The factor of time is more dynamic and changeable than the factor of space. Normally, the factors of space and time can be calculated with a high degree of confidence. On the other hand, the factor of force is often difficult to evaluate properly because of the presence of many elements that are hard or impossible to quantify. A significant change in any of these factors will invariably disturb the overall balance and require a reassessment of all the factors. Hence, the process remains dynamic and the commander should remain alert to detect changes that require reassessment.

c. The factors of space and force in a maritime AO can be balanced by reducing the number or scale of the military objectives to be accomplished. For example, limiting efforts to obtain sea control to a much smaller area or to specific physical media (e.g., surface and air but not subsurface, or surface and subsurface but not air), increasing the number or combat potential of the JFMCC, or reducing the number of ships/aircraft employed in support of other components can achieve this aim. The factors of space and time can also be brought into balance by operating from shorter lines of operation, employing highly mobile forces, deploying maritime forces closer to the scene of potential conflict; pre-positioning weapons/equipment and logistical supplies, reducing the size of the operating area, limiting efforts to obtaining temporary instead of permanent sea control in a given area, achieving operational surprise, conducting military deception, or accepting larger risks.

4. Other General Planning Considerations

a. **Intelligence.** The senior intelligence officers of the maritime component should know their commands intelligence and information requirements and be aware of the priority intelligence requirements (PIRs) of the higher, adjacent, and supporting and subordinate commands, as well as national-level intelligence requirements. JIPOE is the analytical process used by joint intelligence organizations to produce intelligence assessments, estimates, and other intelligence products in support of the commander's decision-making process. The process is used to analyze the physical domains (air, land, maritime, and space); the information environment (which includes cyberspace); political, military, economic, social, information, and infrastructure systems; and all other relevant aspects of the OE; and to determine an adversary's capabilities to operate within that environment. JIPOE products are used to prepare staff estimates, define the OE, describe the impact of the OE on adversary and friendly forces, evaluate the capabilities of adversary forces operating in the OE, and determine and describe potential adversary objectives, COGs, critical vulnerabilities, decision points, COAs, and civilian activities that might impact military operations. The JIPOE effort must be fully coordinated, synchronized, and integrated with the separate intelligence preparation of the battlespace efforts of the component commands and Service intelligence centers. Additionally, JIPOE relies heavily on inputs from several related, specialized efforts, such as geospatial intelligence preparation of the environment and medical intelligence preparation of the OE. All staff elements of the joint force and component commands fully participate in the JIPOE effort by providing information and data relative to their staff areas of expertise. However, JFCs and their subordinate commanders are the key players in planning and guiding the intelligence effort, and JIPOE plays a critical role in maximizing efficient intelligence operations, determining an acceptable COA, and developing a CONOPS. Commanders should integrate the JIPOE process and products into the joint forces planning, execution, and assessment efforts. The process can be applied to the full range of joint military operations (to include civil considerations) and to each level of war. The JIPOE process is described in detail in JP 2-01.3, *Joint Intelligence Preparation of the Operational Environment*.

(1) The JFMCC staff develops a specific collection strategy and posture for each operation to satisfy the commander's critical information requirements (CCIRs), PIRs, and other requirements. JFMCC is also responsible for intelligence support of subordinate forces and intelligence support tasks directed by higher authority. The JFMCC defines tactical-level intelligence responsibilities and prioritizes maritime-related intelligence requirements of tactical forces. The overall intelligence goal is to provide the JFMCC and maritime forces with accurate, timely, and relevant intelligence to support an understanding of the area of influence and area of interest.

(2) The size and composition of the intelligence directorate of a joint staff (J-2) for the JFMCC's staff is dependent upon the joint force maritime component command organization and scope of the operation. Intelligence requirements include access to national, theater, and tactical intelligence systems/data; core analysis capability; ability to provide indications and warnings; ISR collection management skills; targeting capability; and systems and administrative support.

(3) When a Service component commander is designated as a JFMCC, the core intelligence staff normally assumes additional responsibility for operational-level intelligence matters. This can be a significant expansion of the scope of work required to support operational-level staff requirements and decision making, and may require augmentation of the JFMCC's J-2. Augmentation considerations include the nature of the contingency, specific additional skills required to execute the mission, depth of intelligence capability in the existing staff, and additional volume and type of intelligence products required. Figure III-1 reflects skill sets that are typically required to augment the JFMCC's intelligence staff.

b. **Fires and Targeting**

(1) The JFMCC plans, coordinates, synchronizes, and executes joint fires to create lethal or nonlethal effects in order to set the conditions for success in the maritime AO. The JFMCC's focus is on shaping those opponent formations, functions, facilities, and operations that could impact the JFMCC's AO. In addition to providing fires from organic sources, the JFMCC is responsible for synchronizing and integrating all movement and maneuver, fires, and interdiction in support of operations within the maritime AO. Fires typically produce destructive effects; however, various nonlethal means (such as electronic attack) can be employed with little or no associated physical destruction. This function encompasses the fires associated with a number of tasks, missions, and processes, including:

Notional Intelligence Directorate Augmentation Requirements

- Joint targeting systems analysts and weaponeers
- Special security administrators
- Cryptologic resource coordinators and signals-intelligence analysis
- Collection management personnel
- Intelligence analysts
- Imagery exploitation analysts
- Geospatial information analysts
- Intelligence liaison officers (representing each component command and Service)
- Production and dissemination personnel as required (multinational)
- Foreign disclosure personnel
- System administrators to assist with component and multinational support
- Unmanned vehicles support and other intelligence collection platform operators/interpreters
- National intelligence support team
- Joint force counterintelligence and human intelligence staff element

Figure III-1. Notional Intelligence Directorate Augmentation Requirements

(a) Conduct Joint Targeting. This is the process of selecting and prioritizing targets and matching the appropriate response to them, taking account of command objectives, operational requirements, and capabilities.

(b) Provide Joint Fire Support. This task includes joint fires that assist joint forces to move, maneuver, and control territory, populations, airspace, and key waters.

(c) Countering Air and Missile Threats. This task integrates offensive and defensive operations and capabilities to attain and maintain a desired degree of air superiority and FP. These operations are designed to destroy or negate enemy aircraft and missiles, both before and after launch.

(d) Interdict Enemy Capabilities. Interdiction diverts, disrupts, delays, or destroys the enemy's military surface capabilities before they can be used effectively against friendly forces, or to otherwise achieve their objectives.

(e) Conduct Strategic Attack. This task includes offensive action against targets whether military, political, economic, or others which are selected specifically in order to achieve strategic objectives.

(f) Employ information-related capabilities to influence, disrupt, corrupt, or usurp the adversaries decision-making processes.

(g) Assess the Results of Employing Fires. This task includes assessing the effectiveness and performance of fires as well as their contribution to the larger operation or objective.

(2) Fires from maritime platforms can create a range of effects and are a critical component of maritime power projection. Examples of maritime fires employed against targets ashore or over land include interdiction, CAS, suppression of enemy air defenses, counterair (offensive and defensive), and NSFS (direct and general).

(3) The use of fires is one of the principal means of shaping the JFMCC's AO. Information-related capabilities employed to affect adversary information and information systems, are integral to this process. The JFMCC's interests are those adversary forces, functions, facilities, and operations that impact plans and operations.

(4) Joint interdiction operations are a key focus for JFMCC's fires. Fires from maritime assets may be major active elements of interdiction. The key attributes in the JFC's joint interdiction operations are the flexibility, maneuverability and speed of fires assets. Additional information on maritime interdiction can be found in JP 3-03, *Joint Interdiction*.

(5) Concentrated fires, even from dispersed forces, are possible because of the maneuverability of forces and the extended range of their fires. The JFMCC's resources for fires encompass forces assigned by the JFC and may include sea- or shore-based aircraft including fixed- or rotary-wing assigned to theater naval forces, MAGTF, or other aircraft made available for tasking; armed and attack helicopters; surface- and subsurface-launched cruise missiles and torpedoes; surface gunnery, including NSFS; surface-, subsurface- and air-launched mines; air, land, maritime, space, cyberspace, SOF, and unmanned vehicles.

(6) Constant coordination between fires elements will be required. The technical nature of various maritime fires and weapons systems (e.g., programming, guidance, and control procedures) and the fact that a single platform's multiple systems may be supporting numerous commanders in geographically separated areas, and the resultant often complex command relationships, including the nature of support (e.g., direct, general). The JFMCC synchronizes operational fires and C2 by the active participation of the strike and NSFS cell, supporting arms coordination center, and landing force fire support planners, where available, in the planning and targeting processes. Specific JFMCC targeting functions and responsibilities are listed in Figure III-2.

(7) Land and maritime force commanders normally use a four-phase targeting process known as the decide, detect, deliver, and assess (D3A) for fires planning, execution, and interface with the joint targeting cycle. D3A incorporates the same fundamental functions of the joint target cycle. The D3A methodology facilitates synchronizing maneuver, intelligence, and fire support. D3A is not driven by the battle rhythm associated with joint air operations. Components strike targets within their AO with organic capabilities. If the maritime force has insufficient organic assets to strike a target within the maritime AO, or if a maritime target is outside the maritime AO, the targets can be nominated for joint targeting and/or prosecution by another component's assigned forces. Likewise, the maritime force will routinely offer excess strike assets for use in joint missions

Joint Force Maritime Component Commander Targeting Functions and Responsibilities

- Conduct target development.

- Advise the joint force commander (JFC) on the application of maritime operational fires.

- Identify maritime fires support requirements to other components.

- Provide apportionment recommendations to the JFC.

- Recommend joint force maritime component command assets for JFC allocation.

- Advise on joint fires asset distribution and priority of forces.

- Develop priorities, timing, and effects for interdiction within the joint force maritime component commander's (JFMCC's) area of operations (AO).

- Develop JFMCC targeting guidance and priorities.

- Develop a prioritized target nomination list for inclusion in the joint target list, restricted target list, and the no-strike list.

- Nominate targets for inclusion on the JFC's time-sensitive target (TST) list and maintain their own lists of high priority targets.

- Provide appropriate representation to the JFC's joint fires element (JFE) and joint targeting coordination board when established.

- Consolidate and nominate deconflicted and prioritized targets for inclusion in the joint integrated prioritized target list.

- Provide timely and accurate reporting to the JFE in support of joint operations assessment.

- Provide tactical and operational assessment to the JFE for incorporation into the JFC's overall assessment efforts.

- Coordinate components dynamic targeting via established procedures.

- Integrate and deconflict JFMCC fires activity with the JFC and other component commanders or forces.

- Plan, coordinate, and supervise the execution of deep supporting fire operations within the maritime AO.

- Coordinate with designated airspace control authorities for all planned airspace requirements.

- Staff and man the time-sensitive strike branch in the assigned operations cell and ensure TST activity is in accordance with the JFC's TST guidance.

Figure III-2. Joint Force Maritime Component Commander Targeting Functions and Responsibilities

and/or as required by other components. As part of deliberate targeting, the maritime operational commander will coordinate target nominations for the joint target list, no strike list, restricted target list, and maritime prioritized target list for organic strikes in the maritime AO. Use of organic capabilities can help to ensure the maritime operational commander's decision cycle is inside the adversary's. Time sensitive targets (TSTs) and targets of opportunity are usually fleeting with very small windows for weapon engagement.

Commanders and their staffs, in coordination with joint components and other departments and agencies, develop dynamic targeting guidance, which should include priorities and guidance for dynamic targeting and identification of requirements by subordinates; prioritization of targets, including TSTs; guidance for acquisition; TST type and description; desired result; approval authority; acceptable risk; and action against the targets. The commander should articulate risk tolerance sufficiently to let on-scene commanders understand his intent when dynamic targeting requires accelerated coordination. The JFMCC and staff must ensure that dynamic targeting is understood and rehearsed. Components will nominate candidate TSTs, high-payoff targets, and high-value targets during deliberate targeting.

For more information on fires and targeting in the maritime domain, see JP 3-60, Joint Targeting, *and NWP 3-09,* Navy Fire Support.

    c. **Sustainment**

        (1) The sea remains the principal transport medium for large, heavy, and bulky items, as well as large volume requirements. Therefore, maritime logistics capabilities are an important consideration in the development of the JFC's concept of logistics support. The availability of shipping and the ability to transfer supplies ashore, to include the use of joint logistics over-the-shore (JLOTS) capabilities, may influence where and when military operations take place. Additionally, SLOCs and ALOCs may be considered a critical vulnerability and will require continual assessment and protection. The military sealift and merchant marine vessels, which transport the preponderance of the joint force's materiel, remain dependent upon secure ports and airfields in a potential objective area. The sealift operated by our multinational partners varies in its capabilities, while interagency, international organizations, and NGOs are unlikely to possess any form of organic sealift.

        (2) Each Service is responsible for logistic support of its own forces, except as otherwise provided for by agreement with other departments or agencies, multinational partners, or by assignment to a common, joint, or cross-servicing provider. The JFMCC will usually assume logistic coordination responsibilities for all Services and forces operating from a sea base.

        (3) Service component forces are often required to provide significant levels of JOA-wide common-user logistics (CUL) support to other Service components, multinational partners, and other organizations (such as other governmental organizations and NGOs). For the Navy JOA-wide CUL support requirements are normally provided by the parent fleet commanders (i.e., Commander, US Fleet Forces Command and Commander, US Pacific Fleet). However, these requirements are carried out under the auspices of an NCC or a numbered fleet commander and are not a JFMCC's responsibility. US Marine Corps forces may also provide limited CUL support to other Service component forces.

        (4) Authority to direct logistics is not resident in the JFMCC's command authority. However, a CCDR may delegate the authority for the planning, execution and/or management of as many common support capabilities to subordinate commanders as required to accomplish the subordinate commander's objectives. The CCDR must formally

delineate this delegated directive authority by function and scope to the subordinate JFC, Service component commander, or DOD agency. In addition, the JFMCC's CUL authority can be derived from the use of short-term inter-Service support agreements between the Service components.

(5) With this limited CUL authority, the JFMCC can direct CUL support to be provided between Service component units. Operations-focused CUL support is separate and distinct from JOA-wide CUL requirements. This operations-focused CUL can include temporary task organization or the development of support relationships of selected logistic units. The JFMCC's logistic staff monitors and assesses these operations and should coordinate action to prevent conflict or interference with GCC-directed JOA-wide CUL requirements.

(6) Among other functions, the JFMCC's staff coordinates logistics movements and plans to minimize the maneuvers and time required to support resupply of forces at sea. In general, the JFMCC's logistics center manages by exception only. Routine administrative, personnel, and logistics management are the responsibility of the JFC and subordinate Service and component commands.

(7) The ability to conduct at-sea transfer of people and materiel, for both ship-to-ship and ship-to-shore purposes, is a key enabler for deploying, employing, and sustaining joint forces. The foundation of this capability is provided by amphibious ships, aircraft carriers, and military sealift ships. Resources that have reached an initial operating capability like the high-speed intratheater connectors, enhanced surface and air connectors, improved maritime pre-positioning capabilities, and integrated naval logistics should be considered when planning operations and allocating forces. When employed in combination, these capabilities enhance access by reducing the joint force's reliance on ports and airfields in the operational area. Maritime forces have integral logistic support capabilities, including repair and medical facilities that provide individual maritime units and TFs autonomy and the ability to operate for extended periods at considerable distance from shore support.

(8) As crisis, contingency, and major operations result in more demand on existing facilities and increased operational tempo, existing shore-based infrastructure may become inadequate to meet the needed level of support for the increased numbers of units afloat and to Navy and Marine Corps units ashore. The naval advanced logistics support sites and naval forward logistic sites should be expanded to assist in providing required additional support. That expansion is accomplished through the Navy's advanced base functional components (ABFCs). ABFCs are preplanned modular units that provide a variety of functional capabilities to extend the logistic infrastructure supporting naval expeditionary operations. Because of this they can be used to extend shore-based infrastructure as much or as little as needed.

(9) The following provides a non-exhaustive checklist of the JFMCC's logistic planning considerations:

(a) Logistic plans should be integrated with CCDR annexes as well as JFC, Service component, and multinational partner logistic plans.

(b) Logistic personnel must be involved early in the staff planning and undertake an analysis of the logistic support capabilities required for each of the COAs being considered.

(c) CUL requirements must be properly planned and coordinated with JFC-directed CUL requirements.

(d) Logistic personnel should recommend the location and accessibility of key supply points.

(10) The JFMCC is not routinely the lead for JFC-level logistic boards and centers. The JFMCC logistic directorate normally participates on those boards, centers and working groups of critical importance to the success of the maritime portion of the campaign. The theater joint transportation board and the joint movement center, which are transportation-related, may have significant impact on the maritime operations and are examples of higher-level logistic boards on which the JFMCC participates. Among other functions, the JFMCC's staff coordinates and directs logistic plans and movements of assets to minimize the time required to support resupply of forces at sea. Other boards and centers of significant importance to the JFMCC include the joint material priorities and allocation board and the joint petroleum office. For proper focus, JFMCC participation on these boards should be treated as separate and distinct from the Service component participation on these same boards and centers.

(11) The JFMCC does not normally convene separate joint logistic boards and centers except when needed to coordinate critical CUL support within the JFMCC's AO. Possible JFMCC-established boards and centers may include a movement center and materials priorities allocation board.

(12) A JFMCC-level joint movement center is built on the lead Service movement control agency and includes staff members from the other Services. The movement center facilitates coordination and prioritization of movement within the JFMCC's AO, is subordinate to the JFC's joint movement center, and analyzes and prioritizes maritime component movement requirements.

(13) A JFMCC's materials priorities allocation board performs similar functions for critical supply items. The JFMCC can combine the two centers/boards into one distribution management center. The JFMCC, in any case, must ensure that the capability exists to adequately control movement and cross-level critical logistic resources.

(14) The JFMCC's logistic center focuses on key logistic issues that may have an adverse effect on the maritime portion of the joint campaign and in general manages by exception only.

d. **Command and Control Systems Support**

(1) The existing joint theater communications system (TCS) is directed, established, and managed at the CCMD level and provides theater-wide voice and data connectivity between all components and elements. The TCS and nonstandard commercial

systems address unique communications connectivity requirements to provide the appropriate interface between components, multinational forces, interorganizational partners, and C2 that facilitates execution of assigned missions. Tactical communications are phased in and established as specified in the OPLAN or OPORD being executed.

(2) Sensors are key elements in the JFC's communications architecture, with national, theater, and organic component systems all serving as nodes in a joint sensing network. Sensor capability resident in the joint maritime force may support the joint force collection plan and may be integrated into the joint data network. Sensor tasking procedures, allocation of collection assets, and product dissemination should be determined early in the planning process, clearly defined in supporting plans and tactical procedures, and should be adaptable to changing requirements. The JFMCC's staff should access theater and national sensor products to enhance situational awareness, facilitate targeting, and augment organic operational assessment capabilities.

(3) The JFMCC's J-6 provides communications system functional expertise to the JFMCC. The J-6 staff's role is to focus on key communications issues that can have an adverse effect on the JFMCC portion of the campaign, electromagnetic spectrum management, and interference deconfliction. Routine communications system management is the responsibility of the JFC and the subordinate component commands. Communications system hardware is normally a Service component responsibility. However, the JFMCC designates specific force communications functions on an exception basis. Only communications issues affecting the conduct of the operational mission are of concern to the JFMCC's J-6. Guidance to supporting commanders is provided in formal standard operating procedures and OPTASKs.

e. **Protection.** The JFMCC is responsible to the JFC for all aspects of maritime FP. The JFMCC creates FP plans and sets priorities for the forces. FP is a function routinely conducted by maritime forces and essential to mission accomplishment.

f. **Environmental Considerations**

(1) Environmental considerations should be integrated into planning for maritime operations and are included in annex L (Environmental Considerations), as part of the OPLAN. To the extent practicable and consistent with mission accomplishment, commanders should take environmental factors into account during planning, execution, and conclusion of an operation. Commanders should also clearly identify guidance that may be different from the normal practices of the member nations and obtain agreement from participating nations. Besides agreeing on common goals and objectives for the operation, commanders of participating multinational forces should reach some understanding on environmental protection measures during the operation. Failure to accomplish this may result in misunderstandings, decreased interoperability, and a failure to develop and implement a successful environmental annex and plan for the operation. Additionally, the failure to consider environmental impacts on the HN could result in an erosion of support, or acceptance of the operation at home and abroad. Environmental considerations may include those listed in Figure III-3.

Environmental Considerations

- Air pollution from ships, vehicles, aircraft, and construction machinery.
- Cleanup of base camps and other occupied areas to an appropriate level.
- Protection of endangered species and marine mammals in the operational area.
- Environmental safety and health.
- Hazardous materials management.
- Hazardous waste disposal.
- Medical and infectious wastes management and disposal.
- Natural and cultural resources protection.
- Noise abatement, including noise from aircraft operations.
- Pesticide, insecticide, and herbicide management to control non-point pollution.
- Resource and energy conservation through pollution prevention practices.
- Solid waste management and disposal.
- Oil and hazardous substance spills prevention and controls.
- Water pollution from sewage, food service, and other operations.

Figure III-3. Environmental Considerations

(2) Weather has a significant impact on maritime operations and may influence a commander's decision making. Seasonal fluctuations in weather may have strategic significance. Flight operations, amphibious landings, and sonar performance may be made more difficult by high sea states and extreme high or low temperatures. Adverse conditions may also be used to advantage. A submarine, for example, may use poor sonar conditions to avoid detection. The mobility of maritime forces may allow them to move to an operating area where conditions are more favorable. An aircraft carrier may, for instance, seek out and exploit a localized open window in otherwise poor visibility to continue flight operations. This may be a particularly significant capability when shore-based aircraft are weather-bound. Characteristics such as wave height, precipitation, and sea spray impact visibility and radar/sensor effectiveness for platforms and munitions. Ducting, a phenomenon that allows radar energy to travel extended distances within a few hundred feet of the sea surface (under certain conditions), can have a major impact on tactical planning and force positioning.

g. **Law of the Sea**

(1) The oceans of the world traditionally have been classified under the broad headings of internal waters, territorial seas, and high seas. Airspace has been divided into national and international airspace. In the latter half of the 20th century, new concepts evolved, such as the EEZ and archipelagic waters, that dramatically expanded the jurisdictional claims of coastal and island nations over wide expanses of the oceans previously regarded as high seas. The phenomenon of expanding maritime jurisdiction and the rush to extend the territorial sea to 12 nautical miles and beyond were the subject of international negotiation from 1973 through 1982 in the course of the Third United Nations

Conference on the Law of the Sea. That conference produced the 1982 United Nations Convention on the Law of the Sea (UNCLOS) which came into effect on 16 November 1994. In 1983, the US announced that it would neither sign nor ratify the 1982 UNCLOS due to fundamental flaws in its deep seabed mining provisions. Further negotiations resulted in an additional agreement regarding Part XI, which replaced the original deep seabed mining provisions. This agreement contains legally binding changes to the 1982 UNCLOS and is to be applied and interpreted together with the Convention as a single treaty. As of the date of this publication the Senate has not ratified this treaty.

(2) Although the US is not a party to UNCLOS, it considers the navigation and overflight provisions therein reflective of customary international law and thus acts in accordance with UNCLOS, except for the deep seabed mining provisions. President Reagan's 10 March 1983 Oceans Policy Statement provides: first, the US is prepared to accept and act in accordance with the balance of interests relating to traditional uses of the oceans [in the UNCLOS]—such as navigation and overflight. In this respect, the US will recognize the rights of other states in the waters off their coasts, as reflected in the Convention, so long as the rights and freedoms of the US and others under international law are recognized by such coastal states. Second, the US will exercise and assert its navigation and overflight rights and freedoms on a worldwide basis in a manner that is consistent with the balance of interests reflected in the Convention. The US will not, however, acquiesce in unilateral acts of other states designed to restrict the rights and freedoms of the international community in navigation and overflight and other related high seas uses.

(3) The legal classifications ("regimes") of ocean and airspace areas directly affect maritime operations by determining the degree of control that a coastal nation may exercise over the conduct of foreign merchant ships, warships, and aircraft operating within these areas. The nature of these regimes, particularly the extent of coastal nation control exercised in those areas, is set forth in the succeeding paragraphs. The Department of Defense (DOD) 2005.1-M, *Maritime Claims Reference Manual,* contains a listing of the ocean claims of coastal nations. Figure III-4 presents a brief summary of the primary zones affecting navigation and overflight.

h. **Unmanned Aircraft System.** While the C2 processes for unmanned aircraft systems (UASs) are similar to those for manned assets, several characteristics of UASs can make C2 particularly challenging:

(1) UAS communication links are generally more critical than those required for manned systems. In the event of lost communications, a manned aircraft will typically press with the mission or return safely to a home base or alternate field. Although UASs can be programmed to return to base upon loss of communication, they rely on a nearly continuous stream of communications (for both flight control and payload) to successfully complete a mission. Therefore, communications security, and specifically bandwidth protection (from both friendly interference and adversary action) is imperative.

(2) UASs may be capable of transferring control of the aircraft or payloads to multiple operators while airborne. Close coordination amongst all potential operators is required.

Primary Zones Affecting Navigation and Overflight

- Internal waters are landward of the baseline from which the territorial sea is measured.

- The territorial sea is a belt of ocean that is measured seaward up to 12 nautical miles from the baseline of the coastal nation and subject to its sovereignty. Ships enjoy the right of innocent passage in the territorial sea.

- Innocent passage does not include a right for aircraft overflight of the territorial sea.

- A contiguous zone is an area extending seaward from the baseline up to 24 nautical miles in which the coastal nation may exercise the control necessary to prevent or punish infringement of its customs, fiscal, immigration, and sanitary laws and regulations that occur within its territory or territorial sea. Ships and aircraft enjoy high seas freedoms, including overflight, in the contiguous zone.

- An exclusive economic zone (EEZ) is a resource-related zone adjacent to the territorial sea—where a state has certain sovereign rights (but not sovereignty) and may not extend beyond 200 nautical miles from the baseline. Ships and aircraft enjoy high seas freedoms, including overflight, in the EEZ.

- The high seas include all parts of the ocean seaward of the EEZ.

Figure III-4. Primary Zones Affecting Navigation and Overflight

(3) Most larger UASs have considerably longer endurance times than comparable manned systems. Commanders and their staffs should exploit this capability when tasking UAS assets.

(4) Compliance with the airspace control order is critical as unmanned aircraft cannot see and avoid other aircraft, generally have small radar and visual signatures and may not have identification, friend, or foe capability.

5. Assessment

a. Assessment is a process that evaluates changes in the OE and measures progress of the joint force toward mission accomplishment. Commanders continuously assess the OE and the progress of operations; compare them to their initial visualization, understanding, and intent; and adjust operations based on this analysis. Staffs monitor key factors that can influence operations and provide the commander timely information needed for decisions. Normally, the operations directorate of a joint staff (J-3), assisted by the J-2 and the plans directorate of a joint staff (J-5), is responsible for coordinating assessment activities. Various elements of the JFC's staff use assessment results to adjust both current operations and future planning. They are supported by a cross-functional group in the MOC. Within the MOC, the maritime assessment group (MAG) hosts assessment battle rhythm events and develops assessment products. A MAG is composed of a small permanent assessment staff augmented by personnel from the core joint staff areas (intelligence, logistics, etc.) and other functional sections (fires, staff judge advocate, public affairs, IO, etc.) as required. The MAG may also include non-military personnel as appropriate to provide the necessary input and analysis assistance regarding diplomatic, political, military, economic, social, information, and infrastructure systems within the OE.

---

b. Assessment representatives should be active participants in developing and refining effects for MOEs and MOPs as well as visual displays of assessment to portray progress of the operation.

c. The MAG develops the assessment collection plan in concert with the J-2, J-3, and J-5. This plan includes locally produced products that help to organize incoming data for analysis based on information requirements and coordination instructions for conducting evaluations in concert with other staff organizations. The MAG provides assessment information to support J-3 and J-5 planning efforts and recommendations on whether to proceed on course with the current plan or adjust the plan based on execution to date.

d. The assessment process is used to plan, gather, analyze, and interpret MOE data, assessment information from the JFC's staff, other component and staff assessments, and current operations to determine impact on the CONOPS, compliance with commander's intent, and progress on achieving objectives. The MAG is responsible for establishing and updating the assessment picture in order to create a shared situational awareness among the staff, subordinates, and other components. These assessment snapshots support decision making through established battle rhythm events, such as battle or commander's update assessment type briefs, and make recommendations to either "stay the course" or change direction. Assessment efforts are continuous and integrated throughout MOC activities.

e. The JFMCC's MAG should analyze the JFC's desired effects and objectives, develop MOEs and MOPs that apply to the JFMCC, ask for clarifications if necessary, and then integrate assessment measures and activities into the plan. Then ensure any developed MOEs and MOE indicators are consistent with, and not contrary to the JFC's desired effects and objectives.

f. Throughout planning and execution the MAG should be prepared to identify new, desired, or undesired effects. By the time the commander has approved a COA, the MAG should have developed tentative MOEs, sent them to subordinate elements to vet, and addressed and mitigated any inconsistencies. Once the effects, measures, and indicators have been finalized, they should be compared to current CONOPS, CCIRs, and any developed decision support matrices to ensure they are consistent with critical information requirements and anticipated decisions.

6. **Multinational Participation**

a. In a multinational environment, the operational aim for maritime forces is to exercise sea control, project power ashore, synchronize maritime operations with operations throughout the OE, and support the MNFC's CONOPS, intent, and guidance in accomplishing the multinational task force mission. Maritime forces are primarily navies, however, they may include landing forces, maritime-focused air forces, amphibious forces, or other forces charged with sovereignty, security, or constabulary functions at sea that may have the ability to rapidly transition between types of operations. As with land forces, command of maritime operations will normally be assigned to a multinational force maritime component commander (MNFMCC) or a designated TF. The MNFC will typically assign a maritime AO to the MNFMCC or naval TF, based upon the CONOPS. The MNFC will also establish supported and supporting relationships, as required to assist in prioritizing actions, assist in establishing the main effort, and to establish formal command/coordination channels between the components for a specific operation/mission or phase. A key aspect of maritime operations will be sustainability. The following factors will impact the sustainability of maritime operations: available surface ships (combat and amphibious); available submarine assets; maintenance; supply; and storage facilities.

b. Maritime Civil Affairs and Security Training Command personnel can provide assistance to the commander in understanding political and military considerations; language, culture and sovereignty; legal considerations and civil infrastructure of partner nations (PNs) and potential HNs.

For more information on multinational operations, see JP 3-16, Multinational Operations.

CHAPTER IV
COMMAND AND CONTROL AND OTHER OPERATIONAL-LEVEL CONSIDERATIONS FOR SPECIFIC MARITIME OPERATIONS

> *"It is the policy of the United States to take all necessary and appropriate actions, consistent with US law, treaties, and other international agreements to which the United States is a party, and customary international law as determined for the United States by the President, to enhance the security of and protect US interests in the Maritime Domain..."*
>
> **President George W. Bush**
> **December 21, 2004**

1. General

a. While this chapter is not intended as a primer on the conduct of specific maritime operations, due to the complexities of the OE and the required integration and coordination between elements of the joint force, a discussion of selected aspects of specific maritime operations is deemed essential to foster understanding and enhance unified action. The following provides a common baseline for all elements of the joint force to better enable joint planning and facilitate effective JMO.

b. The United States Navy's traditional and doctrinal warfighting configuration is the fleet, commanded by a numbered fleet commander. Typically, the fleet commander task-organizes assigned and attached forces using the Navy's administrative organization as its foundation. This is a historical organizational framework from which extensive warfare doctrine flows. (See Figure IV-1.)

c. The JFMCC may sub-divide the maritime AO and create subordinate TFs, who may in turn create further subordinate organizations. In each case, the establishing authority must designate the command authorities for each subordinate organization, to include support relationships as required. Although the CTF is normally the CWC, the CTF can designate a subordinate commander to be the CWC. CTFs will typically assign forces under TACON to subordinate commanders. A CTF who has OPCON can designate a support command authority between two or more subordinate force commanders.

d. Although a CWC and subordinate warfare and functional group commanders can be assigned in many different ways, for ease of discussion this publication will use composite warfare in the typical context of a strike group comprising multiple varied and multi-mission platforms.

2. Surface Warfare

a. SUW encompasses operations conducted to destroy or neutralize enemy naval surface forces and merchant vessels. These operations typically include the planning and directing of surveillance of the maritime domain, interdiction, and strikes by aircraft and missiles. To facilitate management and promote common understanding, standard

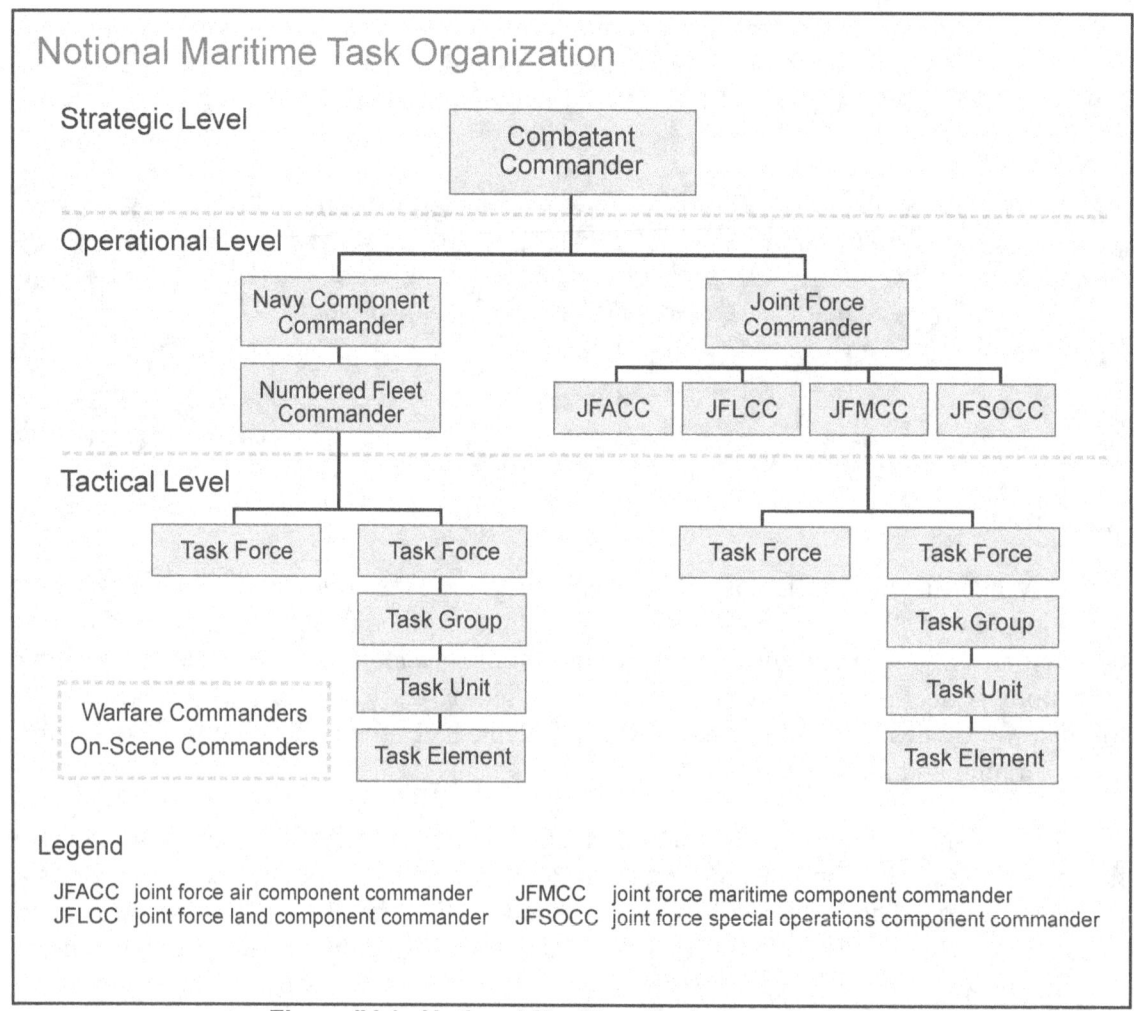

Figure IV-1. Notional Maritime Task Organization

terminology and definitions are used to describe important areas in the maritime AO. The areas described in Figure IV-2 should be clearly delineated in SUW plans, boundaries defined, and specific preplanned responses designated to occur when contacts are present. These designated areas should appear on the COP at tactical and operational levels. JFMCC allocation of capabilities between TFs, assignment of TF responsibilities, maneuver areas, and specific tasking will significantly affect planning for placement of these areas and SUW planning in general.

b. Effective fighting requires aggressive sensor and combat systems management. Effective sensor and combat systems management includes proper modes for sensors and weapons systems; rapid target designation and assignment of targets to weapons systems; use of standard commands and procedures; the ability to launch one's own weapon first and then exploit the tactical advantage gained as the opponent is forced into a defensive posture (subject to rules of engagement [ROE]); employment of sensors to support battle damage assessment; reattack as necessary; designation of a backup system (if available) for each engagement to achieve a higher probability of kill; and consideration of employment of weapons as well as maneuver for defensive countermeasures.

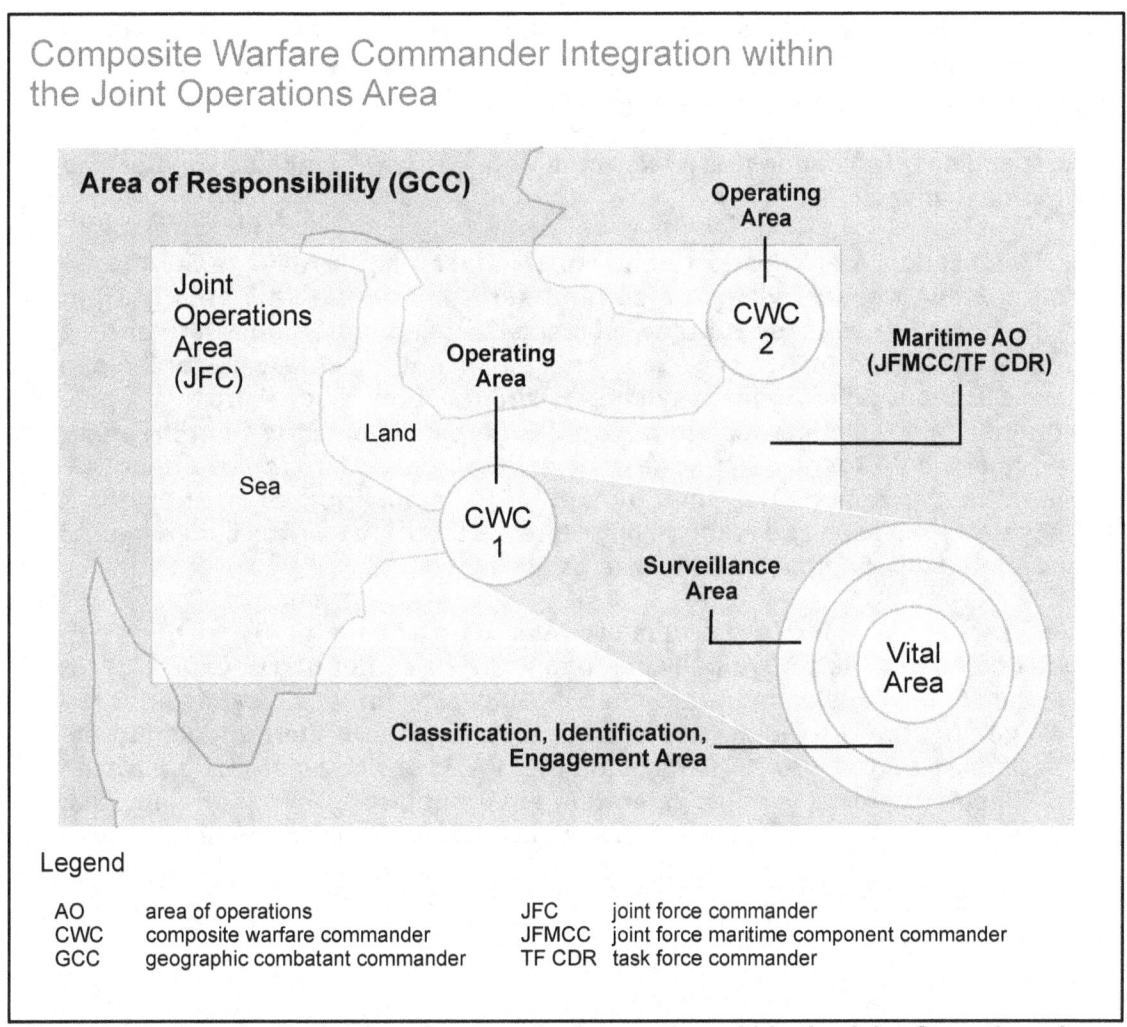

Composite Warfare Commander Integration within the Joint Operations Area

Area of Responsibility (GCC)

Joint Operations Area (JFC)

Operating Area

CWC 2

Operating Area

Operating Area

Land

Sea

CWC 1

Maritime AO (JFMCC/TF CDR)

Surveillance Area

Vital Area

Classification, Identification, Engagement Area

Legend

AO	area of operations	JFC	joint force commander
CWC	composite warfare commander	JFMCC	joint force maritime component commander
GCC	geographic combatant commander	TF CDR	task force commander

Figure IV-2. Composite Warfare Commander Integration within the Joint Operations Area

c. **Tactical Level Surface Warfare Command and Control.** Surface warfare is conducted by the surface warfare commander (SUWC) and the strike warfare commander (STWC). The SUWC will be responsible for defense of the strike group against surface threats. Surface warfare at extended ranges from friendly forces may be assigned to either the SUWC or the STWC. The SUWC typically will:

(1) Exercise TACON of assigned SUW units, including stationing, maneuvering, and engagement.

(2) Identify requirements for SUW air support to CWC.

(3) Establish joining and control procedures for SUW aircraft keeping the air and missile defense commander (AMDC) and appropriate airspace control agencies informed, in accordance with the AMDC's directives.

(4) Order organic strike group aircraft launch and tasking to counter hostile surface contacts.

Surveillance area—The area in the operational environment that extends out to a range equal to the ability of a systematic observation of sensors to detect any aircraft or vessel of possible military concern. The dimensions of the surveillance area are a function of strike group organic surveillance capabilities, indications and warnings sensors, and available theater and national assets.

Classification, identification, and engagement area (CIEA)—The CIEA is the area within the surveillance area (and surrounding the vital area [VA]) in which all contacts should be classified, identified, monitored and, if necessary, escorted, or engaged. The goal is not to destroy all contacts in the CIEA, but rather to make decisions about actions necessary to mitigate the risk that the contact poses. The CIEA typically extends from the outer edge of the VA to the outer edge of where surface warfare forces effectively monitor the operational environment. It is a function of friendly force assets/capabilities and reaction time, threat speed, the warfare commander's desired decision time, and the size of the VA.

Vital area (VA)—The VA is normally centered on a designated area or ship to be defended. The VA typically extends from the center of a defended asset to a distance equal to or greater than the expected threat's weapons release range (WRR). The intent is to engage threats prior to them breaching the perimeter of the VA. The size of the VA is strictly a function of the anticipated threat. In some operating environments, such as the littorals, engaging threats prior to their breaching the VA is not possible because operations are required within the WRR of potential threats. Preplanned responses should include measures for when contacts are initially detected within the VA.

Note: When the aforementioned areas conflict with joint force commander (JFC) established airspace control areas, boundaries will be as coordinated between the joint force maritime component commander and joint force air component commander, or as directed by the JFC and implemented by the JFC's airspace control authority.

d. The SUWC is responsible to the CWC for force action against surface threats. This includes directing MAS and air interdiction of maritime targets (AIMT) within the CIEA. The SUWC collects, evaluates, and disseminates SUW surveillance information, and plans, directs, monitors, and assesses the employment of SUW resources.

For more information on MAS and AIMT, see NTTP 3-20.8/Air Force Tactics, Techniques, and Procedures (Instruction) (AFTTP[I]) 3-2.74, Multi-Service Tactics, Techniques, and Procedures for Air Operations in Maritime Surface Warfare.

e. Typically the SUWC will be embarked in an aircraft carrier, nuclear (CVN), amphibious assault ship (general purpose) (LHA), amphibious assault ship (multipurpose) (LHD) or, if possible, in a ship equipped with a robust Global C2 System-Maritime and cryptologic capabilities to facilitate surface contact management. Due to SUW expertise and experience, a destroyer squadron commander will normally be assigned duties as the SUWC for a CSG. Typically, there is not a destroyer squadron staff assigned to an ARG; therefore, SUWC duties will usually be assigned to the amphibious squadron commander or the commanding officer of the amphibious commander's flagship. The SUWC's staff should be augmented by aviation community representatives, including attack, airborne early warning, ship-based SUW helicopter, and land-based maritime patrol personnel.

3. Air and Missile Defense

a. The JFC, JFMCC, and other component commanders should plan and document preauthorized response actions and delegated command functions in order to enable tactical force commander execution of decentralized operations in the manner expected. The JFC determines the most appropriate command relationships for the component forces made available for counterair. Regardless of the command relationship, all counterair forces are subject to the ROE, airspace control, weapons control measures, and fire control orders established by the joint force air component commander (JFACC), area air defense commander (AADC), or airspace control authority (ACA) as approved by the JFC. Additionally, the AADC will be granted the necessary command authority to deconflict and control engagements and to exercise real-time battle management.

b. For AMD, engagement zones are often established. The zones' designations include who has authority to engage threats and dimensions based upon the capabilities of organic assets. Additional information on engagement zones can be found in JP 3-01, *Countering Air and Missile Threats*. Specific to maritime operations is a self-defense zone (SDZ). An SDZ is a missile engagement zone around an individual surface-to-air capable ship, allowing the ship freedom to take defensive action. The default SDZ is a cylinder around the ship with a 10 nautical mile radius, though each ship's SDZ will be tailored based upon surface-to-air missile capabilities.

c. The maritime force benefits from and contributes to the joint air defense plan using shore-based and organic airborne early warning, fighter aircraft, ships armed with surface-to-air missiles, and electronic warfare systems. The inner layer of defense for a maritime force is provided by a combination of point defense missiles, close-in weapons systems, and electronic countermeasures.

d. When the JFC organizes the joint force, in addition to a JFACC, the JFC also normally designates an AADC (for defensive counterair [DCA]) and an ACA (for joint airspace control). Normally, the JFC designates the same individual as the JFACC, AADC, and ACA, because the three functions are so integral to one another. However, if the situation dictates, the JFC may designate an AADC and/or ACA separate from the JFACC. In that case, the JFC must clearly establish the command relationships of the JFC and the JFACC to the AADC and the ACA.

(1) The JFC designates an AADC with the authority to plan, coordinate, and integrate overall joint force DCA operations. The AADC normally is the component commander with the preponderance of AMD capability and the C2 and intelligence

capability to plan, coordinate, and execute integrated AMD operations, including real-time battle management.

(2) The JFC will define the command relationships between the AADC and other joint force component commanders. Components will provide representatives, as appropriate, to the AADC's HQ to provide both specific weapon systems expertise and broader mission expertise.

For more information on the AADC, see JP 3-01, Countering Air and Missile Threats.

e. When the NCC is designated as the JFMCC ,the JFMCC exercises OPCON of maritime forces to include multi-mission BMD ships. The JFMCC may retain command of multi-mission ships with BMD capability or transfer OPCON or TACON of multi-mission ships with BMD capability to a subordinate CTF. Typically, the CTF integrates AMD when designated. Figure IV-3 contains examples of BMD command functions a JFMCC may assign to a CTF.

f. In the case of maritime air defense regions, the JFMCC may recommend establishing a regional air defense commander (RADC) and a person to fill this position, normally a CTF, to the JFC via the AADC.

g. The AADC, as the supported commander for BMD operations, receives support from other components. The JFMCC operating in support of the AADC for BMD activities prepares maritime BMD capable forces for possible requests for JFMCC support. Figure IV-4 is a visual representation of how a JFC and JFMCC may delegate command relationships and assign command functions for the achievement of BMD mission operational objectives.

h. BMD across the boundary of a GCC's AOR typically is a theater-level operation, with the GCC of the targeted AOR normally the supported commander. Cross-AOR ballistic missile threats are the basis for global planning. Commander, United States Strategic Command is responsible for synchronizing planning for global missile defense and will do so in coordination with other CCMDs, the Services, and as directed, appropriate US Government departments and agencies. Synchronizing and coordination responsibilities, however, do not include authority to execute or direct operations for cross-AOR BMD operations. Each GCC is responsible for BMD in its AOR. Command relationships between GCCs for cross-AOR BMD that address specific AOR threats, international agreements, and partner-nation support requirements are defined by the Secretary of Defense. The JFC's plan should discuss the GCC's support command relationship for the AOR. JFMCC assets that are BMD capable may be tasked to support this effort.

i. Tactical level maritime AMD C2. The AMDC:

(1) Recommends RADC/sector air defense commander assignments to the CWC for submission to/approval by the OTC or JFMCC for follow-on submission to AADC for JFC approval.

(2) Exercises TACON, including stationing and maneuvering of assigned surface AMD capable units.

Examples of Maritime Ballistic Missile Defense
Command Functions

- Assisting with integration of force ballistic missile defense (BMD) plans into the joint force maritime component commander's (JFMCC's) operation plan and, when necessary, providing specific guidance to the force.

- Assisting JFMCC formulation of guidance for BMD planned responses.

- Coordinating and controlling use of maritime BMD sensors.

- Controlling BMD nets, especially with respect to procedural integrity and security in reporting communication security.

- Coordinating and controlling employment of maritime force BMD weapons.

- Defining requirements for protection of multi-mission ships with BMD capability.

- Directing and controlling BMD actions of forces assigned.

- Disseminating criteria for weapon release and expenditure (a matrix if applicable).

- Establishing of JFMCC plans, policies, priorities, and overall requirements for BMD intelligence, surveillance, and reconnaissance activities.

- Exercising command by negation over all BMD actions initiated by other units of the force.

- Exercising tactical control, including stationing and maneuvering of assigned multimission ships with BMD capability, in accordance with the JFMCC's policies and plans.

- Identifying requirements for nonorganic BMD support to the JFMCC.

- Planning and coordinating BMD actions of forces assigned to the JFMCC.

- Recommending BMD degrees of readiness to the JFMCC (note JFMCC cannot set degree of readiness lower than that established by the air and missile defense commander).

- Supporting the task force commander designated by the JFMCC to coordinate integrated air and missile defense operations, or if not assigned, direct liaison with the area and regional air defense commander.

Figure IV-3. Examples of Maritime Ballistic Missile Defense Command Functions

(3) Exercises command by negation over all AMD actions initiated by other units of the force.

(4) Coordinates and orders the launch and station of alert AMD aircraft.

(5) Coordinates movements of friendly aircraft within the air surveillance area in cooperation with the ACA.

(6) Establishes joining procedures for aircraft assigned DCA missions.

(7) Assigns stations, sectors, and/or patrolling areas, and designates air control units for aircraft assigned DCA missions, keeping ACA informed.

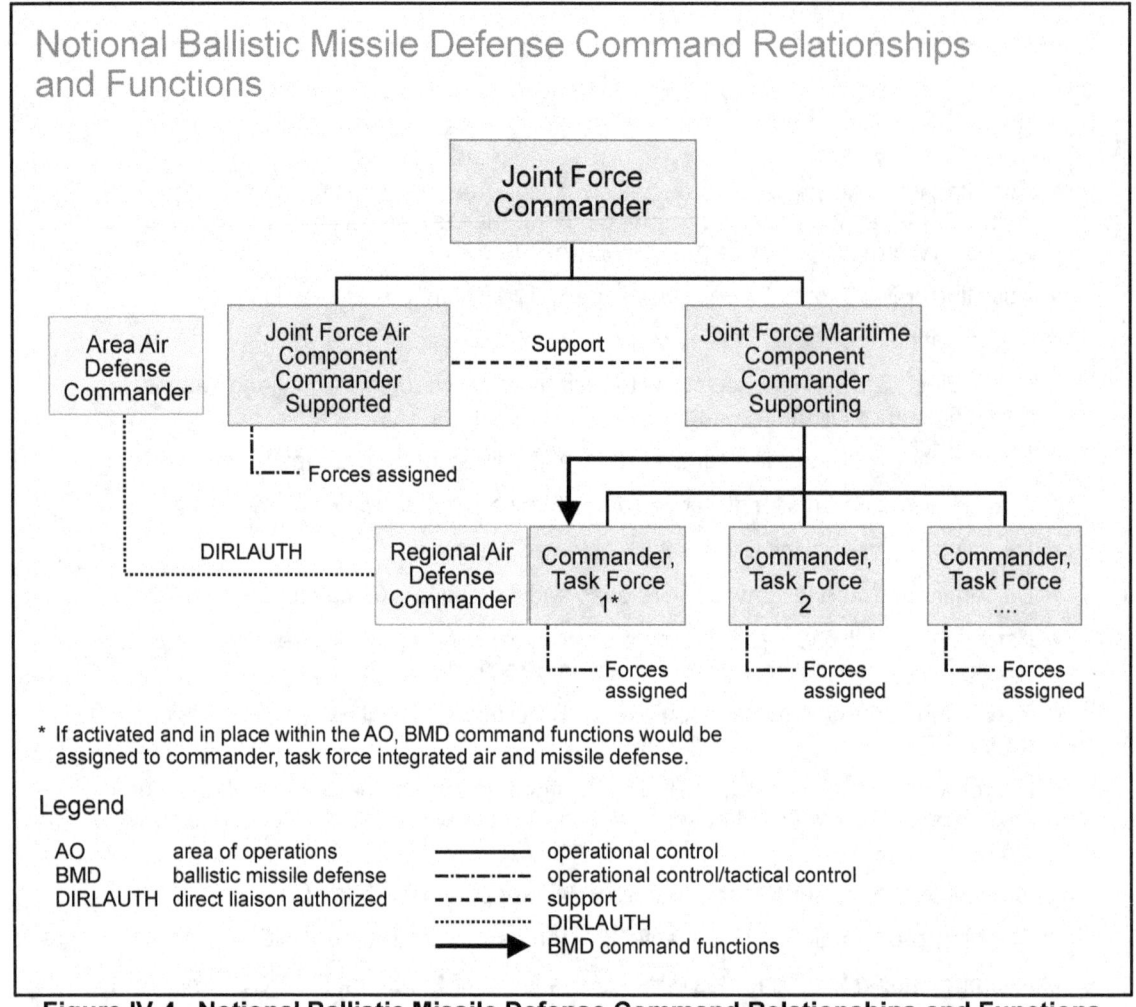

Notional Ballistic Missile Defense Command Relationships and Functions

Joint Force Commander

Area Air Defense Commander

Joint Force Air Component Commander Supported

Support

Joint Force Maritime Component Commander Supporting

Forces assigned

DIRLAUTH

Regional Air Defense Commander

Commander, Task Force 1*

Commander, Task Force 2

Commander, Task Force ....

Forces assigned

Forces assigned

Forces assigned

* If activated and in place within the AO, BMD command functions would be assigned to commander, task force integrated air and missile defense.

Legend

AO	area of operations	————	operational control
BMD	ballistic missile defense	—·—·—·—	operational control/tactical control
DIRLAUTH	direct liaison authorized	- - - - - -	support
		··············	DIRLAUTH
		———→	BMD command functions

Figure IV-4. Notional Ballistic Missile Defense Command Relationships and Functions

(8) In coordination with the ACA, establishes and promulgates the identification safety range and safety sectors for all friendly aircraft and any special areas or zones established for aircraft safety and identification, or to prevent mutual interference.

j. The AMDC is responsible to the CWC for defense of the force against air and ballistic missile threats unless a separate BMD commander has been designated. The AMDC is responsible for collecting, evaluating, and disseminating AMD surveillance information to the CWC and the force, and also plans, directs, monitors, and assesses the employment of AMD resources.

k. The AMDC should be supported by a command center capable of providing sufficient tactical awareness to manage AMD for the force. The AMDC should normally be assigned on the most capable or experienced AMD ship that provides this level of support. Capable ship classes include CG [guided-missile cruiser], DDG [guided-missile destroyer], CVN, LCC [amphibious command ship], LHA, LHD, or LPD [amphibious transport dock]-17. Any component LNOs required, such as an Army air defense artillery fire control officer, would normally embark on the same ship as the AMDC.

l. Platform selection should maximize use of the C2 systems available within the force (e.g., Aegis). Physical space limitations, numbers of watchstanders and their training, the operating environment (e.g., emission control restrictions), and additional command responsibilities should also be used to determine the most capable ship and commander for duties as AMDC.

m. The alternate AMDC should be assigned to a second AMD ship's commanding officer not already assigned warfare or functional group command responsibilities. Similar criteria as discussed for the AMDC should be used when selecting the alternate AMDC.

For additional information regarding AMD, see JP 3-01, Countering Air and Missile Threats.

4. Antisubmarine Warfare

a. Control of the undersea portion of the operational area is vital to the success of joint operations. A principal threat comes from enemy submarines. A single un-located submarine could create a significant operational, diplomatic, or economic impact. To counter this threat, the JFC will coordinate, and when required, integrate assets from the joint force to conduct ASW during all phases of the joint operation or campaign. ASW is an operation conducted with the intention of denying the enemy the effective use of submarines.

b. Although often viewed as a Navy-only mission, the JFMCC may utilize a variety of joint forces and capabilities (air, land, maritime, space, and special operations) to facilitate or conduct ASW. At the operational level of war, ASW will have joint implications. In particular, given the nature of the operating environment, the size of the area to be covered, and the requirement to find, fix, track, target, and engage enemy submarines, the use of persistent national and joint ISR is one of the essential resources to ASW mission accomplishment. For example, the monitoring, tracking, and engagement of enemy submarines in port or transiting on the ocean surface may be effectively accomplished by non-Navy aircraft, UASs, broad area maritime surveillance, or other joint assets.

c. While the JFC is responsible for ASW planning inside the JOA, coordination of ASW plans and activities with commands outside the JOA will be essential and may require close coordination with other government departments and agencies, multinational partners, and HNs.

d. Undersea warfare (USW) operations are conducted to establish dominance in the undersea portion of the maritime domain, which permits friendly forces to operate throughout the OE and denies an opposing force the effective use of underwater systems and weapons. USW includes offensive and defensive submarine, antisubmarine, and MIW operations.

e. ASW is a subset of USW. ASW missions are typically centrally planned under the direction of the JFMCC or a NCC and executed in a decentralized manner in support of the JFC's CONOPS. ASW is extremely complex, requiring the coordination and integration of multiple platforms and systems in order to mitigate the risks posed by enemy submarines.

ASW planning should include consideration of the submarine threat, OE, force planning, ISR, communications systems, and C2.

f. Because it is difficult to detect and track submarines operating underwater, a thorough understanding of the OE is a key tenet of success. Intelligence efforts should focus on the physical attributes of specific enemy platforms, their supporting physical and C2 infrastructure, and past and anticipated employment patterns. Only after a thorough analysis of the physical environment and adversary systems, planners may be able to properly develop the CONOPS.

g. The physical characteristics of the maritime domain have a significant impact on ASW execution. The highly variable acoustic properties of the underwater environment will impact the ability to detect identify, track, and engage enemy submarines. Factors that may affect these properties include surface shipping (including that of the joint force and commercial shipping), inherent environmental noise and oceanographic properties, and seasonal weather patterns. Acoustic sensor placement will be highly dependent on the acoustic properties of the waterspace. Because acoustics will not be the sole detection capability, an environmental assessment will be required to identify the requirements for non-acoustic detection systems (such as satellite imagery).

h. ASW may require joint and combined forces and capabilities. Maritime forces must be identified early to account for long transit times. Initial force planning considerations should include utilization of pre-positioned capabilities, early deployment of surface and subsurface forces, and reassignment of forward deployed forces to the ASW operation. Early presence of joint forces may be essential in seizing the initiative.

i. The objective of ASW operations is to assist in the establishment or maintenance of maritime superiority by denying enemy submarine influence in the operational area. This is accomplished through detection, identification, tracking, and engagement of enemy submarines. Unlocated enemy submarines often have the most influence in the JOA, possibly affecting fleet maneuver and commercial shipping operations. The JFC should designate enemy submarines as TSTs and develop and implement a comprehensive plan to reduce this threat. The operational key to limiting the threat of un-located submarines is to focus the ASW effort to hold enemy submarines at risk and secure friendly maneuver areas.

j. ASW efforts focused on enemy bases and littoral chokepoints can prevent enemy submarines from entering open ocean areas and deny them much of the maritime environment. Neutralizing enemy submarines prior to getting underway, by planned targeting of enemy naval facilities and disrupting critical infrastructure supporting submarine operations is the most effective defense against the enemy submarine threat. Dynamic targeting of enemy submarines may also be possible when the enemy submarine remains on the surface. However, if permitted to enter open ocean areas and submerge, the level of effort required to neutralize the submarine threat increases significantly.

k. Protection of surface units or commercial shipping may require ASW emphasis near operating areas, SLOCs, chokepoints, friendly and neutral ports, or other critical areas.

l. Detection of submarines can have a significant impact on maritime operations. Even if engagement of enemy submarines is prevented by ROE or other considerations, the ability to track enemy submarine movement will shrink the area of influence to the known location of the submarine. The integration of intelligence and operations is essential to the conduct of ASW.

m. The theater antisubmarine warfare commander (TASWC) should maintain direct liaison with the joint intelligence center. Successful ASW prosecution requires fusing intelligence, oceanographic data, surveillance, cueing, multiple sensors, sensor technologies, and coordination between multiple platforms and staffs. Joint and national ISR capabilities must be incorporated into this process.

n. Sensor employment should be thoroughly analyzed and carefully integrated into the CONOPS. Planners must take into consideration the acoustic properties of the operating environment. Sensor platforms should be placed to optimize sensor performance while minimizing the threat to the sensor platform. Acoustics are not the sole detection and tracking mechanism. ISR planning should emphasize that all joint sensors, including those not historically associated with ASW, may provide information for application at both the operational and tactical levels of war.

o. ISR visualization through a common operating picture will maximize MDA and enhance ASW execution. Care must be taken, however, to ensure that the uncertainty inherent in ASW operations is taken into consideration; distinction must be made between suspected location of unlocated submarines and known submarine positions.

p. A survivable, networked joint communications system is essential to facilitate ISR, coordinate multi-platform execution, manage the waterspace, and prevent friendly fire. Information connectivity, exchange, and integration at all levels can help maximize MDA and mission accomplishment.

q. Each GCC operates TASWCs, through the NCC. Each NCC appoints submarine operating authorities (SUBOPAUTHs). The TASWC and SUBOPAUTH closely coordinate submarine operations. In some cases, the TASWC and SUBOPAUTH responsibilities may be shared by a single commander.

r. **Theater ASW Commander.** The TASWC is the commander assigned to develop plans and direct assigned assets to conduct ASW within the CCMD AOR. The TASWC may exercise either OPCON or TACON of assigned and attached assets. When tasked to support a JFC during an operation, the TASWC is normally designated as a TF or task group commander subordinate to the JFMCC. The TASWC conducts ASW operations as permitted by ROE. The TASWC remains responsible to the GCC, outside the subordinate JFC's JOA. The JFC may assign forces directly to the TASWC, or to the JFMCC. The TASWC also directly supports other maritime commanders (i.e., strike group commanders) in the conduct of tactical ASW and typically provides ASW support to afloat forces as they transit through or operate in the AOR. The TASWC should promulgate the WSM and prevention of mutual interference (PMI) elements in effect. As changes to elements of WSM and PMI are promulgated by the SUBOPAUTH, the TASWC should promptly disseminate that information to the force.

s. **Submarine Operating Authority.** The SUBOPAUTH is the Navy commander responsible for ensuring safety, PMI, providing WSM, and controlling the submarine broadcast for assigned submarines within a designated operational area. The SUBOPAUTH may exercise either OPCON or TACON of assigned and attached assets. Within their operational area, SUBOPAUTHs employ WSM to permit the rapid and effective engagement of hostile submarines while preventing inadvertent attacks on friendly submarines. Similar to fire support coordination measures on land, WSM may facilitate reducing or eliminating coordination requirements for the engagement of undersea targets or impose requirements for specific coordination before engagement of targets. Along with other control measures, WSM and associated procedures help ensure that surface and air fires do not jeopardize submarine safety or interfere with other attack means. PMI is waterspace allocation and procedures designed to prevent submerged collision between friendly submarines, between submarines and friendly surface ships' towed bodies, and between submarines and any other underwater event. To effectively employ all available ASW forces and prevent interference with US and multinational submarine forces, the TASWC and SUBOPAUTH must closely coordinate WSM and PMI issues and planning.

t. **Tactical Level ASW Command and Control.** The antisubmarine warfare commander (ASWC) is responsible to the CWC for the defense of the force against submarine threats. The ASWC is normally authorized direct liaison with the SUBOPAUTH and TASWC for the purposes of sharing ASW information and coordination. The ASWC is responsible for collecting, evaluating, and disseminating antisubmarine surveillance information to the CWC and the force, and also plans, directs, monitors, and assesses the employment of antisubmarine resources. The ASWC:

(1) Exercises TACON of assigned surface ASW units and aircraft whose primary mission is ASW, including stationing, maneuvering, and contact prosecution.

(2) Identifies requirements for nonorganic ASW air support to CWC. Establishes the requirements for organic ASW air support.

(3) Provides water space management recommendations to CWC.

(4) Issues specific instructions to all friendly units to prevent mutual interference between submarines in support, towed array surface ships, and all other friendly units.

(5) Orders the launch and employment of alert aircraft to counter the submarine threat.

u. The ASW command center should support temporary installation of acoustic and non-acoustic sensor performance prediction systems tailored to reinforce ASW search operations. Typically, a destroyer squadron commodore embarked on the CWC's flagship is the ASWC. The ASWC's staff is augmented with representatives of the fixed-wing and rotary-wing ASW communities, and naval oceanographic analysis team personnel. When ASW is assigned as the primary mission of submarines operating with a naval force, and if the ASWC is also designated as submarine operations coordination authority, a qualified submarine officer may be assigned to the ASWC to act as submarine element coordinator to achieve required coordination.

v. The alternate ASWC should also be assigned to a destroyer squadron commodore if one is available (e.g., dual carrier operations). If one is not available, an ASW ship's commanding officer not already assigned warfare or functional group command responsibilities should be assigned as the alternate ASWC. Similar criteria as those discussed for the ASWC should be used when selecting the alternate ASWC.

5. Mine Warfare

a. Maritime MIW is divided into two basic subdivisions: the laying of mines to degrade the enemy's capabilities to wage warfare; and the countering of enemy-laid mines to permit friendly maneuver. Environmental considerations play an important role in MIW. Mine cases, mine sensors, target signals, and mine countermeasures (MCM) systems are all affected to some extent by a large number of environmental factors. The basic decisions to hunt or sweep, and subsequent equipment and techniques, are based on an assessment of the environment.

b. Maritime mining is used to support the broad tasks of establishing and maintaining control of essential sea areas. Mines may be employed either offensively or defensively to restrict the movement of surface ships and submarines. They can be used alone to deny free access to ports, harbors, and rivers, as well as movement through SLOCs. Sea mines can also be used as a force multiplier to augment other military assets and reduce the surface and submarine threat.

c. MCM includes all actions undertaken to prevent enemy mines from altering friendly forces' maritime plans, operations, or maneuver. MCM reduces the threat and effects of enemy-laid sea mines on friendly naval force and seaborne logistic force access to and transit of selected waterways. Mine countermeasure operations (MCMOPS) are divided into two broad areas: offensive and defensive MCM.

(1) **Offensive MCM.** The most effective means for countering a mine threat is to prevent the laying of mines, a problem that may require cross-component coordination across the joint force. Offensive MCM destroys enemy mine manufacturing and storage facilities or mine laying platforms before the mines are laid. Although an adjunct of MIW, these operations are not normally conducted by MIW forces. Therefore, staff MCM planners nominate enemy mine layer, mine storage and, ultimately, mine production facilities and assets up through the JFMCC targeting group for inclusion on joint target lists.

(2) **Defensive MCM.** Defensive countermeasures are designed to counter mines once they have been laid. Some measures are undertaken following the termination of conflict solely to eliminate or reduce the threat to shipping posed by residual sea mines. However, most defensive MCMOPS are undertaken during conflict to support (enable) other maritime operations. Defensive MCM includes passive and active MCM.

(a) Passive MCM reduces the threat from emplaced mines without physically attacking the mine itself through reduction of ship susceptibility to mine actuation. Three primary passive measures are practiced: localization of the threat, detection and avoidance of the minefield, and risk reduction.

1. Localization of the threat engenders the establishment of a system of transit routes, referred to as Q-routes, which will be used by all ships to minimize exposure in potentially mined waters. Establishment of transit routes should be one of the first steps taken by MCM planners, if the routes have not been previously designated, to minimize exposure of shipping and permit concentration of active MCM efforts. Minehunting and minesweeping are time consuming operations performed by forces (ships and helicopters) that require localized air and maritime superiority in which to operate. The JFC may need to allocate significant maritime and air forces to protect the MCM force and to prevent the enemy from re-seeding areas already cleared of mines.

2. Detection and avoidance of minefields can be accomplished by exploiting intelligence information or organic MCM forces. When the location has been established, shipping may be routed around the area.

3. Risk reduction is primarily practiced by individual ships rather than planned and executed by MCM forces. Risk may be reduced by controlling the degree of potential interaction with a mine sensor. Against contact mines, a reduction in draft and posting additional lookouts can reduce the number of mines with which the ship's hull might strike. Influence mines can be denied the required activation signals by controlling the ship's emissions. Use of on-board magnetic field reduction equipment or external degaussing, silencing a ship to minimize radiated noise, or using minimum speeds to reduce pressure signature are examples of operational risk reduction. Other types of risk reduction involve the enhancement of ship survivability in the event of mine detonation.

(b) Active MCM are applied when passive measures alone cannot protect traffic. This entails physical interference with the explosive functioning of the mine or actually destroying it. Minehunting and minesweeping are the primary techniques employed in active MCM. Both require detailed intelligence and extensive planning by the MCM commander (MCMC) to counter the threat effectively.

d. Planning and execution of MIW operations, both MCM and mining, require detailed subject matter expertise. For most operations requiring dedicated MCM assets, Commander, Navy Mine and ASW Command, one of the three MCM squadron commanders, or one of the forward-based mine division commanding officers will act as the MCMC. For small-scale operations or those operations employing a single type of MCM asset, the commanding officer or officer in charge from an airborne MCM squadron or explosive ordnance disposal (EOD) mobile unit or detachment may be assigned as the MCMC. When assigned as the mine warfare commander (MIWC), the MCMC is also responsible for planning and executing mining operations. When no MIWC is assigned under the JFMCC, responsibility for planning and executing naval mining operations usually rests with the CWC.

e. The command organization and relationships involving MIW forces will vary for each operation or exercise. In most cases, MIW operations are conducted under the framework of a TF architecture with the MIWC or MCMC reporting directly to the JFMCC. MIW can also be executed under the supported-supporting concept (e.g., the MCMC, operating as MCM TF commander can be assigned as a supporting commander to the amphibious TF commander in support of an amphibious assault).

For additional information regarding MIW, see JP 3-15, Barriers, Obstacles, and Mine Warfare for Joint Operations.

6. Strike Warfare

a. Strike operations may employ ballistic or cruise missiles, aircraft, naval surface fires, Marines and SOF to attack targets ashore. The term "strike warfare" is used in the maritime domain and commonly includes joint fire support, interdiction, strategic attack, and CAS. Amphibious operations may involve extensive application of STW capabilities, while amphibious raids are also a form of strike operations.

b. STW may be conducted by ballistic and cruise missile carrying submarines, aircraft carrier strike aircraft, surface action groups of one or more naval surface vessels with Tomahawk land-attack missiles (TLAMs), naval surface gunnery, rotary-winged aircraft, UAS, and amphibious assault ships. Integration of TLAMs with strike aircraft in the same attack requires close coordination between the airspace coordinating authority, JFACC, JFMCC, and possibly the joint force land component commander to deconflict airspace and target selection. In openly hostile situations, extensive strike operations and offensive application of sea control warfare tasks, particularly with respect to mines and submarines, will be employed to gain access. An important element of gaining access includes neutralizing advanced anti-ship cruise missiles prior to surface forces coming within their range. Long-range, high-speed and maneuvering characteristics of such missiles make in-flight defeat challenging, necessitating strike operations to neutralize adversary launch platforms.

c. The STWC is responsible to the CWC for planning, directing, monitoring, and assessing maritime power projection ashore and may be responsible for striking surface targets at sea at extended ranges from the strike group. The STWC normally exercises TACON of assigned STW assets. Typically, the STWC does not plan or direct TLAM missions. The STWC integrates or coordinates carrier air wing (CVW) resources with TLAM missions via the launch area coordinator and Tomahawk strike coordinator. The STWC coordinates NSFS missions via the NSFS coordinator. The STWC is responsible for identifying requirements for nonorganic STW air support.

d. The STWC should have direct access to the CWC, key strike planning personnel, and the intelligence center. Typically, a CVW commander embarked on the CWC's flagship is the STWC for CSGs. The amphibious squadron commodore is normally the STWC for ARGs. The staff of the STWC should include air wing representation from each of the different capability areas, cruise missile and NSFS officer augmentation, and intelligence support. The STWC will normally provide LNOs to the JFACC as part of the naval and amphibious liaison element.

7. Amphibious Operations

Amphibious operations are complex and normally involve all components of the joint force. It is typified by close integration of forces trained, organized, and equipped for different combat functions. The JFC and JFMCC should ensure that the amphibious objective area or operational area is shaped by CSGs and other maritime and joint assets in anti-access/area denial environments prior to the commencement of the amphibious operation. Shaping operations include establishing maritime and air superiority, which is necessary for the amphibious operation to occur. The supporting relationship between the CSGs and other joint forces conducting the shaping operations and the amphibious force should be determined and provided in an establishing directive. Fundamental principles and guidance on the planning and execution of amphibious operations, to include command relationships and logistic support requirements are contained in JP 3-02, *Amphibious Operations.* Doctrine for the embarkation and debarkation of the landing force conducting amphibious operations can be found in JP 3-02.1, *Amphibious Embarkation and Debarkation.* NATO doctrine ratified by the US can be found in AJP-3.1, *Allied Joint Maritime Operations.* Additional allied tactics, techniques, and procedures can be found in ATP-8, *Amphibious Operations.*

8. Naval Surface Fire Support

a. NSFS units are normally OPCON to the NCC or TACON to the JFMCC and provide direct or general support to other joint force components or subordinate forces of the JFMCC (e.g., an amphibious force). When supporting a landing force or other ground forces, an NSFS spotting team is usually attached to the maneuvering forces for fire support coordination purposes.

b. For NSFS of an amphibious assault, when the number of ships permits, each assault battalion will be assigned a ship in direct support. The ship delivers fires in the zone of fire (ZF), which normally corresponds to the zone of action of the supported unit. When possible, ships capable of performing simultaneous missions will be given multiple direct support missions to allow for maximum support to the landing force.

c. A ship in general support attacks targets in the ZF which correspond to the zone of action of the supported unit. Prearranged fires are delivered in accordance with a schedule of fires published in the amphibious TF OPORD and the NSFS plan in the landing force OPORD. Fires may also be allocated to a subordinate unit for a specific mission(s). Upon completion of the mission(s), the ship reverts to general support. Ships in general support are paired with regimental-sized units or larger.

9. Information Operations

a. IO planning occurs at the operational level (e.g., JFMCC, NCC) while execution occurs at the tactical level normally under the direction of a strike group or ARG commander.

b. The JFMCC plans actions in the information environment that disrupt and degrade adversary decision making and C2 systems, while protecting their own decision making and C2 systems. The JFMCC sets the conditions and creates the environment to allow tactical units to successfully execute IO tasks. The IO cell focuses on a range of disciplines and functions to develop a coordinated IO plan. The IO cell consists of the IO cell lead and subject matter experts on the use of information-related capabilities to achieve the commanders information related objectives. Communications between the JFC and the JFMCC may be difficult because of the geographic separation of the commands. The JFMCC should normally send a LNO to the JFC's IO cell to facilitate communications and provide details on employment of maritime IO forces and capabilities. Upon receipt and analysis of the JFC's mission statement, the IO planning cell must pass any details of ongoing IO themes and shaping efforts to the JFC and other component commanders' IO planners. The LNO can be instrumental in providing the IO cell with the necessary information, and assistance where required.

c. **Tactical Level Information Operations Command and Control.** The IO warfare commander is responsible to the CWC to shape and assess the information environment; achieve and maintain information superiority; develop and execute IO plans in support of CWC objectives; and support other warfare commanders.

For additional information regarding IO, see JP 3-13, Information Operations, *and NTTP 3-13.1,* Theater and Campaign Information Operations Planning.

10. Maritime Interception Operations

a. MIO are efforts to monitor, query, and board merchant vessels in international waters to enforce sanctions against other nations such as those in support of United Nations Security Council resolutions (UNSCRs) and/or prevent the transport of restricted goods. Boarding teams of Sailors, Marines, Coastguardsmen, and specialized law enforcement personnel are trained in the techniques of visit, board, search, and seizure (VBSS) to conduct MIO worldwide. These boardings are used for specific missions based on authorities, laws, and jurisdiction. US warships may be tasked to conduct MIO or to provide support to embarked forces tasked with conducting boardings that are beyond the capability of normal ship's force VBSS teams. As in any operation, commanders considering opposed or noncompliant boardings (NCBs) must have timely intelligence of the threat and associated degree of risk and weigh this against the benefits of apprehension and capabilities of the forces to be employed.

b. MIO lines of authority should be streamlined, and must be clearly understood by all forces involved in the conduct of the mission. The command structure selected may vary but typically will include some form of a support relationship, with the embarked forces being the supported command and other forces being in a supporting role; not withstanding that the maritime interception operations commander (MIOC) continues to be the officer assigned to command the operation (i.e., maintain TACON).

c. Expanded MIO are authorized by the President and directed by the Secretary of Defense to intercept vessels identified to be transporting terrorists and/or terrorist-related material that pose an imminent threat to the US and its allies.

d. Historically, MIO is a peacetime measure designed to enforce embargoes sanctioned by the United Nations Security Council (UNSC), national authority, or other regional organization. However, the line between peacetime MIO and belligerent rights during international armed conflict can become blurred. Purely peacetime MIO share many operational characteristics with the exercise of belligerent rights; however, they are conceptually different. The use of lethal force is closely controlled during MIO and is used only where necessary as a measure of last resort when all other means of embargo enforcement, to include nonlethal means, have failed. The recognized sanctioning body establishes the provisions of MIO (e.g., in a UNSCR). After a CCDR responsible for conducting MIO is designated, an OPORD is issued that conforms to the resolution. The NCC may issue AO specific OPTASK supplements that address:

(1) The materials to be identified, tracked, diverted, or seized.

(2) The disposition of identified goods that are not to enter or leave a specified nation.

(3) The types of suspect vessels expected to transit the operational area.

(4) The questions to ask the suspect vessel during boarding.

(5) The criteria for diversion.

(6) The percentages of cargo that should be searched on each type of ship.

(7) ROE.

(8) The criteria used for classifying contacts and determining cleared vessels from possible sanction violators.

(9) The reporting procedures for initial contact report, boarding summaries, challenge summaries, diversion reports, and after action reports.

e. The conduct of MIO missions is based upon the concept of assessing the physical characteristics and level of resistance anticipated or known to exist on the unit to be boarded versus the abilities of the boarding team. Boarding are characterized as compliant boarding, NCB, and opposed boarding. When embarking on a suspect vessel via helicopter insertion during an NCB or when opposed specially trained and equipped forces are required. Each boarding is unique and inherently risky. A compliant boarding can quickly degrade into an NCB or opposed situation for a variety of reasons, a significant planning factor.

f. Traditionally the primary mechanism for initiation of MIO has been through a UNSCR; however, other authorizations include the consent of a coastal state or flag state, the consent of the master of a vessel, an interception as a condition of port entry, the belligerent right of visit and search, the interception of a stateless vessel, or an interception made pursuant to the right of self-defense. The authority to engage in MIO is based on international law and is given by the UNSC, national authority, or other regional authority. Once it is decided the US will participate in an operation, authorization for US forces to conduct MIO missions is initiated by the Secretary of Defense after approval by the President. The Chairman of the Joint Chiefs of Staff designates the appropriate CCDR to perform MIO based on the geographic location of operations. Depending on the nature and location of the threat, national level leadership of federal departments and agencies other than DOD may participate in the development and approval of courses of action to respond to maritime threats through the MOTR plan. MOTR is a component plan of the national strategy for maritime security. The US is party to Proliferation Security Initiative (PSI) agreements with a number of other countries. These PSI agreements, entered into in furtherance of UNSCR 1540, provide legal authority for the parties to board each other's vessels when such vessels are suspected of transporting weapons of mass destruction (WMD), their delivery systems, and related materials. In response to WMD proliferation in the maritime domain, DOD conducts MIO in accordance with the standing Maritime Counterproliferation Interdiction Execute Order.

g. USCG law enforcement detachments (LEDETs) may be embarked on various vessels for boardings associated with MIO, specifically, for counterdrug (CD) operations against drugs coming into the US. Law enforcement in accordance with Title 14, US Code, Section 89, gives the USCG statutory authority to make inquiries, examinations, inspections, searches, seizures, and arrests upon the high seas and waters over which the US has jurisdiction for the prevention, detection, and suppression of violations of the laws of the US. MIO by warships is authorized under international law to support international policy objectives. Navy ships carrying LEDETs support federal law enforcement efforts, but Navy and other DOD personnel are generally prohibited from direct involvement in law enforcement activity, such as boarding in conjunction with LEO, arrest, or seizure. Such personnel may fill support functions including damage control, gas-free engineering, liquid load transfer, use of warning shots and/or disabling fire (while under USCG TACON), jettisoned contraband recovery, and interpreting. CD operations and alien migrant interdiction operations are examples of LEO. LEO by USCG personnel, including LEDETs, are governed by the USCG Commandant, United States Coast Guard, Instruction M16247.1, *Maritime Law Enforcement Manual (MLEM)*. The USCG MLEM includes detailed guidance with respect to legal authorities and policy (including USCG use of force policy) for USCG law enforcement missions.

h. **Tactical Level MIO Command and Control.** As directed by the JFMCC, the MIOC or OTC will normally be designated as the primary authority for VBSS within the AO and gives the authority to conduct boardings, designates the supporting ships, air assets, and support teams (e.g., LEDET, EOD, and search and rescue), provides all available intelligence products, assigns communications frequencies required, and designates the on-scene commander (OSC) who will exercise TACON of the VBSS operation. The MIOC or OTC may assume the responsibilities of OSC and exercise TACON of all the forces and assets. The OSC assumes TACON, conducts surveillance, maintains accurate position data, and provides essential elements of information on the suspect vessel. The OSC reports progress of the operation to the MIOC and decides whether to go ahead with the mission or abort.

For further information on MIO, see NTTP 3-07.11, Maritime Interception Operations.

11. Maritime Security Operations

a. Maritime security includes a collection of tasks that are derived from agreed-upon international law. MSO are those operations conducted to assist in establishing the conditions for security and protection of sovereignty in the maritime domain. Examples of MSO include missions to counter maritime-related terrorism, weapons proliferation, transnational crime, piracy, environmental destruction, and illegal seaborne immigration. These tasks include assisting mariners in distress, participating in security cooperation operations with allies and partners, sharing situational awareness, and conducting maritime interception and LEO. MSO involve close coordination among governments, the private sector, international organizations, and NGOs.

b. Maritime forces, acting in concert with other joint and multinational forces, other government departments and agencies, and law enforcement agencies employ the following options in response to maritime threats: increased surveillance and tracking, MIO, LEO, expanded MIO, and environmental defense operations.

c. **Piracy.** International law has long recognized a general duty of all nations to cooperate in the repression of piracy. Piracy is an international crime consisting of illegal acts of violence, detention, or depredation committed for private ends by the crew or passengers of a private ship or aircraft beyond the territorial sea of another nation against another ship or aircraft or persons and property on board (depredation is the act of plundering, robbing, or pillaging). In international law, piracy is a crime that can be committed only on or over the high seas, EEZ, and contiguous zone, and in other places beyond the territorial jurisdiction of any nation. The same acts (e.g., armed robbery, hostage taking, kidnapping, extortion) committed in the internal waters, territorial sea, archipelagic waters, or national airspace of a nation do not constitute piracy in international law but are, instead, crimes within the jurisdiction and sovereignty of the littoral nation.

d. Only warships, military aircraft, or other ships or aircraft clearly marked and identifiable as being in governmental service may seize a pirate ship or aircraft. A pirate vessel or aircraft, and all persons on board, seized and detained by a US vessel or aircraft should be taken, sent, or directed to the nearest port or airfield and delivered to appropriate law enforcement authorities for disposition, as directed by higher authority.

e. If a pirate vessel or aircraft fleeing from pursuit by a warship or military aircraft proceeds from the contiguous zone, EEZ, high seas, or international airspace, into the territorial sea, archipelagic waters, or national airspace of another country, every effort should be made to obtain the consent of the nation having sovereignty over the territorial sea, archipelagic waters, or superjacent airspace to continue pursuit. The inviolability of the territorial integrity of sovereign nations makes the decision of a warship or military aircraft to continue pursuit into these areas without such consent a serious matter. However, in extraordinary circumstances where life and limb is imperiled and contact cannot be established in a timely manner with the coastal nation, or the coastal nation is unable or unwilling to act, pursuit may continue into the territorial sea, archipelagic waters, or national airspace. US commanders should consult applicable standing ROE and OPORDs for specific guidance. Pursuit must be broken off immediately upon request of the coastal nation, and, in any event, the right to seize the pirate vessel or aircraft and to try the pirates devolves on the nation to which the territorial seas, archipelagic waters, or airspace belong.

f. Pursuit of a pirate vessel or aircraft through or over international straits overlapped by territorial seas or through archipelagic sea lanes or air routes may proceed with or without the consent of the coastal nation or nations, provided the pursuit is expeditious and direct and the transit passage or archipelagic sea lanes passage rights of others are not unreasonably constrained in the process.

g. **Tactical Level Maritime Security Operations Command and Control.** C2 considerations for MSO vary depending upon the nature of the mission although they parallel those for MIO. VBSS tactics will typically be employed during these missions.

12. Maritime Expeditionary Security Operations

A maritime expeditionary security force (MESF) is organized as an adaptive security force package supporting the JFMCC in providing all-weather, day and night security in the transition from the sea base inland, green to brown water, and ashore. The maritime expeditionary security force commander (MESFC) is that officer designated to conduct MESF operations within a designated coastal geographic area. The MESFC usually exercises OPCON over assigned MESF units, as directed, and may delegate TACON of these forces for coastal sea control and harbor operations to subordinate commanders. Control of forces will typically be further delegated to a seaward security officer (typically for riverine operations, port security unit operations, and salvage services) and a landward security officer (for EOD, maritime civil affairs and security training, and naval construction services).

For further information on MESO, see NWP 3-10, Maritime Expeditionary Security Operations.

13. Maritime Homeland Defense, Defense Support of Civil Authorities, Maritime Operational Threat Response Plan

a. **Homeland Defense.** Securing the maritime approaches is essential to keeping the homeland safe. DOD maritime assets must be able to detect, identify, localize, evaluate, sort, and when warranted, intercept or interdict threats to prevent or defeat an attack. This is a complex task as adversaries may not be easily differentiated from normal maritime activity, and any disruption of commercial trade may have economic and financial implications domestically and internationally. It is also critical for DOD to maintain unrestricted freedom of movement to ensure the ability to deploy forces overseas. Responding to unpredictable transnational threats requires coordination across the US Government to prevent attacks on the homeland. Coordination and interoperability with federal, state, tribal, and law enforcement agencies (LEAs), particularly the USCG, US Customs and Border Protection, and the Federal Bureau of Investigation, are important in this effort due to overlapping authorities, responsibilities and potential simultaneous presence of response assets for maritime operations in the conduct of homeland defense (HD). Additionally, sharing of information and cooperation with multinational partners in regards to global maritime activities will greatly assist in the early detection and subsequent interception of maritime threats.

b. Defense support of civil authorities (DSCA) operations include support of US civil authorities for major disasters, emergencies, civil disturbance operations, designated defense support of civilian law enforcement authorities, and domestic special events.

c. DOD, through the relevant CCDR, is prepared to respond to maritime threats from the forward regions to the homeland. DOD maritime forces support an active layered defense through extensive operations in the forward regions, coupled with a high state of readiness and scalability to varying threat conditions in the maritime approaches and homeland. DOD plays the lead role in a maritime HD construct, where DOD is identified as the federal agency with lead responsibility whether it is by discovery of a threat during normal operations, which requires immediate action, or through the protocols established by the MOTR Plan. These protocols are based on existing law, desired US Government outcome, greatest potential magnitude of the threat, response capabilities required, asset availability, and authority to act. During a DOD HD operation, USCG assets may also be under the control of a CCDR to defeat the threat to the homeland. Conversely, if it is determined to be a Department of Homeland Security mission, US Navy assets could come under TACON of the USCG.

d. The *National Strategy for Maritime Security* and the MOTR Plan are directed in the NSPD-41/HSPD-13, *Maritime Security Policy*. The MOTR Plan establishes the protocols to achieve coordinated, unified, timely and effective planning and execution by various departments and agencies of the US Government. The MOTR plan addresses the full range of maritime security threats to the homeland including nation-state military threats; piracy; state/non-state criminal, unlawful or hostile acts such as smuggling; threat vessels with cargo or personnel requiring investigation and disposition.

e. The MOTR plan predesignates US Government departments and agencies with lead responsibilities, clarifies interagency roles and responsibilities, and establishes protocols and procedures that are utilized for a coordinated response to achieve the US Government's desired outcome for a particular threat.

f. The MOTR protocols and procedures allow rapid response to short-notice (pop-up) threats and require interagency partners to begin coordination activities (i.e., MOTR conference calls) at the earliest possible opportunity when one of the following triggers are met:

(1) Any specific terrorist or state threat exists, and US response action is or could be imminent.

(2) More than one US Government department or agency has become substantially involved in responding to the threat.

(3) The agency or department either lacks the capability, capacity, or jurisdiction to address the threat.

(4) Upon resolving the threat, the initial responding US Government department or agency cannot execute the disposition of cargo, people, or vessels acting under its own authority.

(5) The threat poses a potential adverse effect on the foreign affairs of the US.

g. The MOTR coordination process is conducted through a virtual network of interagency national and operational command centers. This coordination process is the key element in determining which agency is the right choice for leading the US Government response and what other departments and agencies are needed to support the response effort. Additionally, the MOTR protocols include a process for transition of the lead from one agency to another and dispute resolution (i.e., if the US Government desired outcome cannot be resolved at the lower levels of government, the characterization of a particular threat could ultimately be elevated for resolution by higher authority). At the tactical level, it is important to realize that the MOTR process exists not only to achieve a US Government desired outcome, but to coordinate and assist in bringing additional capabilities to bear on a threat.

h. Additionally, MOTR presents guiding principles that apply to all agencies at all times and sets the basic standards for interagency actions to overcome maritime threats to the US.

i. Successful MOTR execution is fundamentally reliant on the operational intelligence linkage. This linkage is optimized through ongoing efforts to achieve MDA.

For additional information regarding HD, see JP 3-27, Homeland Defense, *and for more information on DSCA see JP 3-28,* Defense Support of Civil Authorities*. More information on the different authorities and requirements between USCG Title 14, USC, and USN Title 10, USC, during maritime operations can also be found in both publications.*

14. Global Maritime Partnerships, Security Cooperation, and Global Fleet Stations

a. Global maritime partnerships, security cooperation and global fleet stations represent the overarching framework by which the US Government fosters and sustains cooperative relationships with international maritime partners. In concert with other Services, other US Government departments and agencies, NGOs, and private industry, the Navy, Marine Corps, and Coast Guard address mutual maritime concerns such as freedom of navigation, the safe flow of commerce, deterrence of terrorism, and protection of the oceans' resources in a voluntary, informal, and nonbinding capacity. Global fleet stations are an enabler of the global maritime partnership initiative. US maritime forces engage with like-minded nations to enhance security and governance. This is normally accomplished through mutual security training to expand the number of maritime professionals, assist nations in developing maritime awareness, infrastructure, law enforcement expertise, and the ability to respond to maritime threats and challenges. Building partner capacity and capability is achieved through information exchange, training and exercise opportunities, multinational operations, and interoperability enhancements.

b. Naval forces provide the means of maintaining a global military presence while limiting the undesired economic, social, political, or diplomatic repercussions that often accompany US forces based ashore. Culturally aware forward deployed naval forces can provide a stabilizing influence on regional actors and can prevent or limit conflict. Forward naval forces provide US policy makers a range of options for influencing events while minimizing the risk of being drawn into a crisis or protracted entanglement.

c. Theater security cooperation tasks may include the use of maritime civil affairs, riverine, construction, EOD, mobile diving, intelligence, logistics, medical, and training resources. Maritime forces may also employ security cooperation MAGTFs to build partner capacity and enhance civil-military operations. The USCG's deployable operations group, comprised mostly of maritime safety and security teams with specific, specialized training, brings together various specialized incident response, law enforcement and security teams into adaptive force packages for surge operations which can deploy in advance of a potential conflict to conduct prevention activities or after a conflict has ensued to compliment conventional forces and contribute to establishing and sustaining stability.

d. Global fleet stations, such as the Africa Partnership Station initially deployed in 2007, have been established to support the GCC's security cooperation and engagement activities. They are best described as highly visible, positively engaged, persistent sea bases of operations from which to interact with PN military and civilian populations and the global maritime community.

e. Domestic civil law enforcement and port security expertise are uniquely valuable today as CCDRs work to build foreign nation capacity for security and governance. In recent years, CCDRs have requested USCG forces to conduct interception and antipiracy operations, foreign liaison, and other supporting tasks.

15. Seabased Operations

a. A sea base provides a JFC with a scalable and mobile capability in the JOA from which to exercise C2 or provide strike, power projection, fire support, and logistics capabilities where and when needed. A sea base can be as small as one ship, or it can expand to consist of dozens of ships. Seabasing minimizes the need to place vulnerable assets ashore and a sea base can be established without reliance on HN support. A sea base may be composed of forces drawn from each joint force component. Seabasing is predicated on the ability to attain local maritime superiority. Discrete and tailored, sea-based forces are often deemed preferable among the local populace and government as a less obtrusive support option compared to having foreign troops on the ground in their country.

b. **Command and Control of Seabased Operations.** The command relationships established to conduct operations from the sea base are shaped by the mission requirements and will follow established joint doctrine command relationships. The sea base will typically be aligned under the JFMCC or the NCC. The JFMCC may designate a subordinate OTC to enable delegation of seabasing tasks as needed to manage the span of control commensurate to the mission(s) assigned, size, scope, threat environment, and availability of forces.

c. **Other Considerations for Seabased Operations.** An overriding objective of seabased operations is to position scalable, tailorable, and employable maritime or joint forces at sea within the JOA to seize the initiative in order to respond to mission tasking. Accordingly, the end state is the point in time when a commander determines that sufficient personnel and equipment resources have closed on the operational area in preparation to carry out assigned tasks. It is the responsibility of the JFMCC to coordinate with a JFC to ensure the seabasing time-phased force and deployment data (TPFDD) and request for forces requirements are integrated with the overall TPFDD, to enable support to all components of the sea base.

d. Determine that seabasing will or will not be used to meet mission objectives. Consider all tools available to meet commander's intent. Be cognizant of the principles and limitations of seabasing and how they may apply to meeting operational objectives. Seabasing may contribute to the commander's operational objectives by using the sea as maneuver space; leveraging forward presence and joint interdependence; protecting joint/multinational force operations; providing scalable, responsive joint power projection; sustaining joint force operations from the sea; expanding access options and reducing dependence on land bases; and creating uncertainty for adversaries. Some seabasing considerations are included in Figure IV-5.

e. Once a decision has been made to establish a sea base and to define the capabilities and capacities that must be present in the sea base to meet commander's intent, the following questions should be addressed:

(1) What surveillance and FP capabilities are required in order to achieve and maintain access within the air and surface environments and to enable freedom of movement and maneuver for all seabasing lines of operation in support of mission objectives?

(2) What surveillance and FP capabilities are required within the maritime environment to extend naval defensive capabilities throughout the JOA to protect joint forces operating at sea and ashore?

(3) What detection and FP capabilities are required in order to provide adequate defense against attacks by naval surface forces, submarines, small boats, and asymmetric terrorist or suicide attacks from surface craft and swimmers?

(4) In the event of mines, what capabilities are required to detect, identify, neutralize, or clear mines to ensure maneuver access across key littoral approaches?

f. In order to determine if conditions have been met that no longer require seabasing capabilities or applications, the following questions should be posed and answered:

(1) Are aerial ports of debarkation (APOD) and/or seaports of debarkation (SPOD) capable of supporting continued military deployment, employment, sustainment, and reconstitution?

(2) Is FP sufficient?

Seabasing Considerations

- What is the capacity that the aerial port of debarkation facility can support?
- What are the number of available berths, adequacy of piers (cranes, road access, etc.), as well as draft pier side that the seaport of debarkation can support?
- What are the environmental issues such as fire/debris?
- Will political, diplomatic, and cultural environments within the operational area impact the scale and type of military operation?
- Will the local geography/hydrography and estimated threat support military operations and sustainment using seabased assets?
- Can seabased assets provide sufficient maritime protection; be dispersed widely enough to minimize susceptibility?
- How will weather impact seabased operations (to include sea state)?
- Can seabase operate 24 hours per day/7 days per week?

Figure IV-5. Seabasing Considerations

(3) Is there an internal transportation network available?

(4) Post APOD and/or SPOD establishment operations ashore may warrant the sea base remain. Will throughput be sufficient to support operational needs?

(5) Does the sea base provide additional flexibility, security, or additional distribution capability?

g. JFMCC's C2 tasks include:

(1) Planning and executing the support of required plans for assigned missions.

(2) Coordinating planning efforts with higher, lower, adjacent, and multinational HQ, as required.

(3) Developing maritime COAs within the framework of a JFC-assigned objective or mission, forces available, and the commander's intent.

(4) Determining maritime forces required and available and coordinating deployment planning in support of the selected COAs.

(5) Developing and integrating the maritime component communications systems architecture and plans that support the JFC's operational requirements.

(6) Directing and controlling the execution of operations conducted by maritime forces.

h. The information infrastructure for the sea base will be an integral part of the larger joint C2 infrastructure. It is the underlying foundation that enables the free flow of

---

information throughout all levels of the command structure. The sea base information infrastructure should provide an interoperable and scalable integrated C2 infrastructure supporting a common, standardized set of joint and multinational C2 capabilities, integrated applications, and hardware. The information infrastructure should enhance the ability to rapidly activate and deploy a sea base with a common package that can sustain operations for the duration of the contingency, support efficient routing of distributed C2 through collaborative networks, and decrease the lag between deployment and full operational capabilities.

i. The command relationships established to conduct operations from the sea base are shaped by the mission requirements and should follow established joint doctrine. A JFC can C2 operations through subordinate joint TFs, Service components, functional components, or a combination of Service and functional components. The sea base will typically be aligned under the JFMCC when assigned. The JFMCC is responsible for operational C2 and is the single focal point for integrating and synchronizing maritime operations.

j. Seabasing of SOF encompasses a wide spectrum of activities. Naval special warfare (NSW) forces to include NSW combatant craft have the capability to rendezvous with ships at sea via parachute.

For more information refer to NTTP 3-07.11.1, Surface Ships in Support of Naval Special Warfare Operations.

16. Counterdrug Operations

a. GCCs are responsible for planning and executing DOD CD operations within their AORs. DOD supports federal, state, and local LEAs in their effort to disrupt the transport and/or transfer of illegal drugs into the US. CD is a high priority national security and international cooperation mission, with DOD functions and responsibilities based on statutory authority. The Armed Forces of the US also assists our PNs in their CD efforts.

b. The C2 relationships established for CD operations will vary based on the environments in which they are conducted. Considering that most CD operations are in support of either PNs or LEAs, it is important to remember that even though command of US military forces will remain within DOD, the overall control of the mission may be determined by a lead federal agency or agreements with foreign authorities.

c. Joint maritime forces can play an important role in ISR, interdiction, lift, and sustainment operations

For additional information regarding CD operations, see JP 3-07.4, Counterdrug Operations.

17. Noncombatant Evacuation Operations

Joint maritime forces, especially amphibious forces, are often used to conduct noncombatant evacuation operations (NEOs). This is primarily due to their forward deployed posture; ability to maintain forces afloat, thus not taxing the infrastructure ashore or raising tensions around the US mission or toward US presence; an ability to provide additional forces should the security situation warrant; their self-sustainability, and the ability to transition to other types of operations or provide access for the deployment of other forces. Additional information on NEOs may be found in JP 3-68, *Noncombatant Evacuation Operations.*

18. Protection of Shipping

a. There are multiple methods and options to protect shipping. One method is to conduct wide sea control operations that attempt to protect the waters or known traffic routes through which many ships pass. Another method is to gather merchant ships and devote protection assets to the convoy, requiring only localized supremacy. Both constructs can be used within wider sea control operations if resources permit. When there is a severe risk to maritime trade, convoying is a method of reducing the scale of the sea control problem that has, in the past, proved effective. If shipping is gathered in convoys, the area and time over which sea control must be exercised for their protection is reduced to a minimum. Convoying complicates the attacker's task and concentrates escorting forces to enhance the effectiveness of protection. However, convoying is less likely to deceive the enemy or deny the enemy intelligence about the position of friendly shipping. It presents the enemy a much more localized and lucrative target. It is also disruptive to trade. The strategic or operational decision to convoy requires careful weighing of advantages, disadvantages, and the opportunities for drawing the enemy into decisive action.

b. During any operation, merchant ship activity needs to be closely monitored, and effective coordination and close cooperation between military, civilian, commercial, and government organizations is required to provide for the necessary level of liaison and safety. In certain situations, maritime forces may be called upon to protect ships of any nationality carrying cargoes of interest to the US and its allies. NATO created the NCAGS that established an organization and procedures to provide continuous near real-time situational awareness of merchant shipping in support of maritime HD and the forward deployed theater/operational commanders. NCAGS provide accurate and timely merchant vessel information and advice on the deconfliction and protection of the vessels in the AOR. The NCAGS mission bridges the gap between operational forces and merchant shipping by providing a framework for communicating directions, advisories, concerns, and information. The range of options is designed to allow flexibility in tailoring NCAGS policy to the particular requirements and situation in the NCAGS area. In its simplest form, NCAGS is another tool to support the operational commander's overall sea control mission requirement, directed and managed as any other warfare mission area asset.

c. NCAGS doctrine has evolved with the changing threat posed both on merchant shipping and by merchant shipping in the context of regional operations and maritime HD. This doctrine addresses both the traditional protection and control of shipping in a region and the emerging requirement of maritime HD, where merchant shipping may be either the protagonist, or target, requiring the establishment of communications to increase maritime situational awareness of merchant shipping. NCAGS doctrine applies to maritime HD, contingency support, and general economic shipping. Maritime HD support encompasses assisting the USCG and fleet commanders with increasing MDA by contributing to the production of a COP relating to merchant shipping within the territorial seas and EEZ waters surrounding the US, its territories, and interests. Types of contingency support shipping include naval vessels of the Military Sealift Command, shipping operated or chartered by the US Government to support naval operations or to meet US policy objectives, crisis response shipping, and relief shipping chartered by government departments or agencies. Types of economic shipping include vessels engaged in normal commercial trade worldwide, regardless of flag or ownership, or such other shipping that is not under the control or direction of the US Government.

d. Specific to maritime HD operations in the United States Northern Command (USNORTHCOM) AOR, the USCG is the lead Department of Homeland Security agency for maritime security. The MOCs work jointly with the USCG maritime intelligence fusion centers to form the joint maritime information fusion center. The MOCs are responsible to assist in improving MDA by providing positional information of merchant vessels operating in the USNORTHCOM AOR.

19. Maritime Pre-Positioning Force Operations

a. A maritime pre-positioning force (MPF) operation includes the airlift of MAGTF and Navy elements, the Navy support element, and naval port security units with selected equipment into an arrival and assembly area to join with equipment and supplies carried aboard maritime pre-positioning ships. An MPF operation may consist of one ship interacting with a forward-deployed MEU; a maritime pre-positioning ships squadron (MPSRON) and a Marine expeditionary brigade fly-in echelon; or a Marine expeditionary force falling in on the MPSRONs. The MPF is one component of the Marine Corps' rapid response capability triad, which also includes the air contingency MAGTF and forward-deployed amphibious forces.

b. An MPF is a temporary organization comprised of a MAGTF with assigned naval forces under the MAGTF command element, and an MPSRON, NAVFOR, and naval forces under the command of the commander, maritime pre-positioned force (CMPF). The command relationship established between the MAGTF commander and the CMPF is a key decision. It should provide for unity of effort, simplicity, and flexibility across the MPF operation phases. It should be clearly defined and based upon an assessment of mission requirements. The support relationship is normally established between the CMPF and MAGTF commander. For MPF operations, the Navy support element would consist of Navy Expeditionary Logistics Support Group (NAVELSG) forces actually off-loading the MAGTF cargo and interfacing between the MPSRON vessels and the deployed MEU. For the MAGTF, NAVELSG forces support the loading and unloading of cargo and passengers. If JLOTS becomes part of the sustainment or assault follow-on echelon operations, NAVELSG forces will be providing logistics support in many areas.

For additional information regarding maritime pre-positioning operations, see Marine Corps Warfighting Publication (MCWP) 3-32/NTTP 3-02.3M, Maritime Prepositioning Force Operations, *and JP 4-01.2,* Sealift Support to Joint Operations.

20. Foreign Humanitarian Assistance

Maritime forces can provide speed of reaction, operational maneuver, and assured access while significantly reducing the footprint ashore and minimizing the permissions required to operate from the HN. Forward deployed ARGs with an embarked MEU provide immediate national response in support of humanitarian and natural-disaster relief operations. This includes MAGTF response teams, platoon-sized elements capable of detecting a wide range of chemical, biological, radiological, and nuclear hazards. Other forward deployed maritime units, including CSGs, individual ships or cutters, and deployed US naval construction force units may provide more limited immediate relief support, including airlift support, personnel recovery, engineering capabilities such as bridging and debris removal, and providing a secure platform for staging or rest and recuperation until a larger force arrives. US Navy ships can provide a safe and accessible location for the JFC's HQ, provide seabasing support to the joint force, and have a limited ability to produce and distribute electrical power and clean water. Riverine forces, expeditionary training teams, hospital ships, expeditionary medical facilities and forward deployable preventive medicine units are other US Navy assets that can be tailored to support FHA missions. The Marine Corps MPF is another resource strategically located around the world that may respond to a regional crisis that involve FHA and disaster relief. These ships have the capability to purify water and transfer it ashore. Bulk petroleum, oils, and lubricants transfer capability is also available.

21. Defense Support of Civil Authorities

Humanitarian tasks also are included in DSCA. In response to request for assistance from civil authorities, maritime forces can support whole-of-government responses to domestic emergencies.

For more information on DSCA, see JP 3-28, Defense Support of Civil Authorities.

APPENDIX A
REFERENCES

The development of JP 3-32 is based upon the following primary references:

1. General

    a. NSPD-41/HSPD-13, *Maritime Security Policy.*

    b. The National Strategy for Maritime Security.

2. Chairman of the Joint Chiefs of Staff Publications

    a. JP 1, *Doctrine for the Armed Forces of the United States.*

    b. JP 1-0, *Joint Personnel Support.*

    c. JP 1-02, *Department of Defense Dictionary of Military and Associated Terms.*

    d. JP 2-0, *Joint Intelligence.*

    e. JP 2-01, *Joint and National Intelligence Support to Military Operations.*

    f. JP 2-01.3, *Joint Intelligence Preparation of the Operational Environment.*

    g. JP 3-0, *Joint Operations.*

    h. JP 3-01, *Countering Air and Missile Threats.*

    i. JP 3-02, *Amphibious Operations.*

    j. JP 3-03, *Joint Interdiction.*

    k. JP 3-07.2, *Antiterrorism.*

    l. JP 3-09, *Joint Fire Support.*

    m. JP 3-10, *Joint Security Operations in Theater.*

    n. JP 3-13, *Information Operations.*

    o. JP 3-13.3, *Operations Security.*

    p. JP 3-15, *Barriers, Obstacles, and Mine Warfare for Joint Operations.*

    q. JP 3-16, *Multinational Operations.*

    r. JP 3-28, *Defense Support of Civil Authorities.*

s. JP 3-29, *Foreign Humanitarian Assistance.*

t. JP 3-30, *Command and Control for Joint Air Operations.*

u. JP 3-31, *Command and Control for Joint Land Operations.*

v. JP 3-33, *Joint Task Force Headquarters.*

w. JP 3-52, *Joint Airspace Control.*

x. JP 3-57, *Civil-Military Operations.*

y. JP 3-59, *Meteorological and Oceanographic Operations.*

z. JP 3-60, *Joint Targeting.*

aa. JP 4-0, *Joint Logistics.*

bb. JP 4-01, *The Defense Transportation System.*

cc. JP 4-01.2, *Sealift Support to Joint Operations.*

dd. JP 4-01.5, *Joint Terminal Operations.*

ee. JP 4-01.6, *Joint Logistics Over-the-Shore (JLOTS).*

ff. JP 4-09, *Distribution Operations.*

gg. JP 5-0, *Joint Operation Planning.*

3. Multi-Service Publications

a. Field Manual 90-41/Marine Corps Reference Publication 5-1A/NWP 5-02/AFTTP(I) 3-2.21, *Multi-Service Tactics, Techniques, and Procedures for Joint Task Force (JTF) Liaison Operations.*

b. NTTP 3-20.8/AFTTP(I) 3-2.74, *Multi-Service Tactics, Techniques, and Procedures for Air Operations in Maritime Surface Warfare.*

c. NTTP 3-02.3M/ MCWP 3-32, *Maritime Prepositioning Force Operations.*

d. NWP 3-62M/MCWP 3-31.7, *Seabasing.*

4. Navy Publications

a. NTTP 3-13.1, *Theater and Campaign Information Operations.*

b. NTTP 3-32.1, *Maritime Operations Center.*

c. NTTP 4-01.4, *Underway Replenishment*.

d. NTTP 4-02.1, *Medical Logistics*.

e. NTTP 4-02.2, *Patient Movement*.

f. NTTP 4-02.7, *Health Service Support in a Chemical, Biological, Radiological, and Nuclear Environment*.

g. NTTP 4-04.1, *Seabee Operations in the MAGTF*.

h. NTRP 4-10.1, *Naval Conventional Ordnance Management*.

i. NWP 2-01, *Intelligence Support to Naval Operations*.

j. NWP 3-09, *Navy Fire Support*.

k. NWP 3-10, *Maritime Expeditionary Security Operations (MESO)*.

l. NWP 3-13, *Navy Information Operations*.

m. NWP 3-15 Series, *Mine Warfare*.

n. NWP 3-20 Series, *Surface Warfare*.

o. NWP 3-21 Series, *Antisubmarine Warfare*.

p. NWP 3-32, *Command and Control of Maritime Forces at the Operational Level of War*.

q. NWP 4-01, *Naval Transportation*.

r. NWP 4-01.1, *Navy Advanced Base Logistics Operations*.

s. NWP 4-08, *Naval Supply Operations*.

t. NWP 4-09 Rev A, *Other Logistic Services*.

u. NWP 4-11, *Environmental Protection*.

v. NWP 5-01 Rev A, *Naval Operational Planning*.

Intentionally Blank

APPENDIX B
ADMINISTRATIVE INSTRUCTIONS

1. User Comments

Users in the field are highly encouraged to submit comments on this publication to: Joint Staff J-7, Deputy Director, Joint and Coalition Warfighting, Joint and Coalition Warfighting Center, ATTN: Joint Doctrine Support Division, 116 Lake View Parkway, Suffolk, VA 23435-2697. These comments should address content (accuracy, usefulness, consistency, and organization), writing, and appearance.

2. Authorship

The lead agent for this publication is the US Navy. The Joint Staff doctrine sponsor for this publication is the Joint Staff Operations Directorate (J-3).

3. Supersession

This publication supersedes JP 3-32, 08 August 2006, Change 1, 27 May 2008, *Command and Control for Joint Maritime Operations.*

4. Change Recommendations

a. Recommendations for urgent changes to this publication should be submitted:

TO: JOINT STAFF WASHINGTON DC//J7-JEDD//

b. Routine changes should be submitted electronically to the Deputy Director, Joint and Coalition Warfighting, Joint and Coalition Warfighting Center, Joint Doctrine Support Division and info the lead agent and the Director for Joint Force Development, J-7/JEDD.

c. When a Joint Staff directorate submits a proposal to the Chairman of the Joint Chiefs of Staff that would change source document information reflected in this publication, that directorate will include a proposed change to this publication as an enclosure to its proposal. The Services and other organizations are requested to notify the Joint Staff J-7 when changes to source documents reflected in this publication are initiated.

5. Distribution of Publications

Local reproduction is authorized, and access to unclassified publications is unrestricted. However, access to and reproduction authorization for classified JPs must be IAW DOD Manual 5200.01, Volume 1, *DOD Information Security Program: Overview, Classification, and Declassification,* and DOD Manual 5200.01, Volume 3, *DOD Information Security Program: Protection of Classified Information.*

6. Distribution of Electronic Publications

a. Joint Staff J-7 will not print copies of JPs for distribution. Electronic versions are available on JDEIS at https://jdeis.js.mil (NIPRNET) and http://jdeis.js.smil.mil (SIPRNET), and on the JEL at http://www.dtic.mil/doctrine (NIPRNET).

b. Only approved JPs and joint test publications are releasable outside the CCMDs, Services, and Joint Staff. Release of any classified JP to foreign governments or foreign nationals must be requested through the local embassy (Defense Attaché Office) to DIA, Defense Foreign Liaison/IE-3, 200 MacDill Blvd., Joint Base Anacostia-Bolling, Washington, DC 20340-5100.

c. JEL CD-ROM. Upon request of a joint doctrine development community member, the Joint Staff J-7 will produce and deliver one CD-ROM with current JPs. This JEL CD-ROM will be updated not less than semi-annually and when received can be locally reproduced for use within the CCMDs and Services.

GLOSSARY
PART I—ABBREVIATIONS AND ACRONYMS

AADC	area air defense commander
ABFC	advanced base functional component
ACA	airspace control authority
AFTTP(I)	Air Force tactics, techniques, and procedures (instruction)
AIMT	air interdiction of maritime targets
AJP	allied joint publication
ALOC	air line of communications
AMD	air and missile defense
AMDC	air and missile defense commander
AO	area of operations
AOC	air operations center
AOR	area of responsibility
APOD	aerial port of debarkation
ARG	amphibious ready group
ASW	antisubmarine warfare
ASWC	antisubmarine warfare commander
ATP	allied tactical publication
BMD	ballistic missile defense
C2	command and control
CAS	close air support
CCDR	combatant commander
CCIR	commander's critical information requirement
CCMD	combatant command
CD	counterdrug
CIEA	classification, identification, and engagement area
CJCSM	Chairman of the Joint Chiefs of Staff manual
CMPF	commander, maritime pre-positioned force
COA	course of action
COG	center of gravity
CONOPS	concept of operations
COP	common operational picture
CSG	carrier strike group
CTF	commander, task force
CUL	common-user logistics
CVN	aircraft carrier, nuclear
CVW	carrier air wing
CWC	composite warfare commander
D3A	decide, detect, deliver, and assess
DCA	defensive counterair
DOD	Department of Defense

DSCA	defense support of civil authorities
EEZ	exclusive economic zone
EOD	explosive ordnance disposal
FHA	foreign humanitarian assistance
FP	force protection
GCC	geographic combatant commander
HD	homeland defense
HN	host nation
HQ	headquarters
HSPD	homeland security Presidential directive
IO	information operations
ISR	intelligence, surveillance, and reconnaissance
J-2	intelligence directorate of a joint staff
J-3	operations directorate of a joint staff
J-5	plans directorate of a joint staff
J-6	communications system directorate of a joint staff
JDDOC	joint deployment and distribution operations center
JFACC	joint force air component commander
JFC	joint force commander
JFMCC	joint force maritime component commander
JIPOE	joint intelligence preparation of the operational environment
JLOTS	joint logistics over-the-shore
JMO	joint maritime operations
JOA	joint operations area
JOPP	joint operation planning process
JP	joint publication
LEA	law enforcement agency
LEDET	law enforcement detachment (USCG)
LEO	law enforcement operations
LHA	amphibious assault ship (general purpose)
LHD	amphibious assault ship (multipurpose)
LNO	liaison officer
LOC	line of communications
MAG	maritime assessment group
MAGTF	Marine air-ground task force
MAS	maritime air support
MCM	mine countermeasures
MCMC	mine countermeasures commander

MCMOPS	mine countermeasures operations
MCWP	Marine Corps warfighting publication
MDA	maritime domain awareness
MESF	maritime expeditionary security force
MESFC	maritime expeditionary security force commander
MESO	maritime expeditionary security operations
MEU	Marine expeditionary unit
MIO	maritime interception operations
MIOC	maritime interception operations commander
MIW	mine warfare
MIWC	mine warfare commander
MLEM	Maritime Law Enforcement Manual
MNFC	multinational force commander
MNFMCC	multinational force maritime component commander
MOC	maritime operations center
MOE	measure of effectiveness
MOP	measure of performance
MOTR	maritime operational threat response
MPF	maritime pre-positioning force
MPSRON	maritime pre-positioning ships squadron
MSO	maritime security operations
NATO	North Atlantic Treaty Organization
NAVFOR	Navy forces
NCAGS	naval cooperation and guidance for shipping
NCB	noncompliant boarding
NCC	Navy component commander
NGO	nongovernmental organization
NSFS	naval surface fire support
NSPD	national security Presidential directive
NTTP	Navy tactics, techniques, and procedures
NWP	Navy warfare publication
OE	operational environment
OPCON	operational control
OPLAN	operation plan
OPORD	operation order
OPTASK	operation task
OSC	on-scene commander
OTC	officer in tactical command
PIR	priority intelligence requirement
PMI	prevention of mutual interference
PN	partner nation
PSI	Proliferation Security Initiative

RADC	regional air defense commander
ROE	rules of engagement
SCC	shipping coordination center
SDZ	self-defense zone
SLOC	sea line of communications
SOF	special operations forces
SPOD	seaport of debarkation
STANAG	standardization agreement (NATO)
STW	strike warfare
STWC	strike warfare commander
SUBOPAUTH	submarine operating authority
SUW	surface warfare
SUWC	surface warfare commander
TACON	tactical control
TASWC	theater antisubmarine warfare commander
TCS	theater communications system
TF	task force
TLAM	Tomahawk land-attack missile
TPFDD	time-phased force and deployment data
TST	time-sensitive target
UAS	unmanned aircraft system
UNCLOS	United Nations Convention on the Law of the Sea
UNSC	United Nations Security Council
UNSCR	United Nations Security Council resolution
USCG	United States Coast Guard
USNORTHCOM	United States Northern Command
USW	undersea warfare
VBSS	visit, board, search, and seizure
WMD	weapons of mass destruction
WSM	waterspace management
ZF	zone of fire

aircraft carrier. A warship designed to support and operate aircraft, engage in attacks on targets afloat or ashore, and engage in sustained operations in support of other forces. Also called **CV** or **CVN.** (Approved for incorporation into JP 1-02.)

antisubmarine warfare. Operations conducted with the intention of denying the enemy the effective use of submarines. Also called **ASW.** (Approved for incorporation into JP 1-02 with JP 3-32 as the source JP.)

antisubmarine warfare forces. None. (Approved for removal from JP 1-02.)

area operations. None. (Approved for removal from JP 1-02.)

at sea. None. (Approved for removal from JP 1-02.)

battle force. None. (Approved for removal from JP 1-02.)

carrier air wing. Two or more aircraft squadrons formed under one commander for administrative and tactical control of operations from a carrier. Also called **CVW.** (Approved for incorporation into JP 1-02.)

carrier strike group. A standing naval task group consisting of a carrier, embarked air wing, surface combatants, and submarines as assigned in direct support, operating in mutual support with the task of destroying hostile submarine, surface, and air forces within the group's assigned operational area and striking at targets along hostile shore lines or projecting power inland. Also called **CSG.** (Approved for incorporation into JP 1-02 with JP 3-32 as the source JP.)

composite warfare commander. An officer to whom the officer in tactical command of a naval task organization may delegate authority to conduct some or all of the offensive and defensive functions of the force. Also called **CWC.** (Approved for incorporation into JP 1-02 with JP 3-32 as the source JP.)

contiguous zone. 1. A maritime zone adjacent to the territorial sea that may not extend beyond 24 nautical miles from the baselines from which the breadth of the territorial sea is measured. 2. The zone of the ocean extending 3-12 nautical miles from the United States coastline. (Approved for incorporation into JP 1-02.)

defensive sea area. None. (Approved for removal from JP 1-02.)

force rendezvous. None. (Approved for removal from JP 1-02.)

forward presence. Maintaining forward-deployed or stationed forces overseas to demonstrate national resolve, strengthen alliances, dissuade potential adversaries, and enhance the ability to respond quickly to contingencies. (Approved for inclusion in JP 1-02.)

general quarters. None. (Approved for removal from JP 1-02.)

global fleet station. A persistent sea base of operations from which to interact with partner nation military and civilian populations and the global maritime community. Also called **GFS.** (Approved for inclusion in JP 1-02.)

global maritime partnership. An approach to cooperation among maritime nations with a shared stake in international commerce, safety, security, and freedom of the seas. Also called **GMP.** (Approved for inclusion in JP 1-02.)

marine environment. None. (Approved for removal from JP 1-02.)

maritime control area. None. (Approved for removal from JP 1-02.)

maritime domain. The oceans, seas, bays, estuaries, islands, coastal areas, and the airspace above these, including the littorals. (JP 1-02. SOURCE: JP 3-32)

maritime domain awareness. The effective understanding of anything associated with the maritime domain that could impact the security, safety, economy, or environment of a nation. Also called **MDA.** (Approved for incorporation into JP 1-02.)

maritime forces. Forces that operate on, under, or above the sea to gain or exploit command of the sea, sea control, or sea denial and/or to project power from the sea. (JP 1-02. SOURCE: JP 3-32)

maritime power projection. Power projection in and from the maritime environment, including a broad spectrum of offensive military operations to destroy enemy forces or logistic support or to prevent enemy forces from approaching within enemy weapons' range of friendly forces. (Approved for incorporation into JP 1-02.)

maritime security operations. Those operations to protect maritime sovereignty and resources and to counter maritime-related terrorism, weapons proliferation, transnational crime, piracy, environmental destruction, and illegal seaborne immigration. Also called **MSO.** (Approved for inclusion in JP 1-02.)

maritime superiority. That degree of dominance of one force over another that permits the conduct of maritime operations by the former and its related land, maritime, and air forces at a given time and place without prohibitive interference by the opposing force. (JP 1-02. SOURCE: JP 3-32)

maritime supremacy. None. (Approved for removal from JP 1-02.)

nautical mile. None. (Approved for removal from JP 1-02.)

naval base. None. (Approved for removal from JP 1-02.)

naval operation. 1. A naval action (or the performance of a naval mission) that may be strategic, operational, tactical, logistic, or training. 2. The process of carrying on or training for naval combat in order to gain the objectives of any battle or campaign. (JP 1-02. SOURCE: JP 3-32.)

numbered fleet. A major tactical unit of the Navy immediately subordinate to a major fleet command and comprising various task forces, elements, groups, and units for the purpose of prosecuting specific naval operations. (Approved for incorporation into JP 1-02 with JP 3-32 as the source JP.)

officer in tactical command. In maritime usage, the senior officer present eligible to assume command, or the officer to whom the senior officer has delegated tactical command. Also called **OTC.** (Approved for incorporation into JP 1-02 with JP 3-32 as the source JP.)

on berth. None. (Approved for removal from JP 1-02.)

open ocean. Ocean limit defined as greater than 12 nautical miles from shore, as compared with high seas that are over 200 nautical miles from shore. (Approved for incorporation into JP 1-02.)

perils of the sea. None. (Approved for removal from JP 1-02.)

piracy. None. (Approved for removal from JP 1-02.)

prevention of mutual interference. In submarine operations, procedures established to prevent submerged collisions between friendly submarines, between submarines and friendly surface ship towed bodies and arrays, and between submarines and any other hazards to submerged navigation. Also called **PMI.** (Approved for incorporation into JP 1-02.)

riverine area. None. (Approved for removal from JP 1-02.)

riverine operations. Operations conducted by forces organized to cope with and exploit the unique characteristics of a riverine area, to locate and destroy hostile forces, and/or to achieve or maintain control of the riverine area. (Approved for incorporation into JP 1-02.)

sea control operations. The employment of forces to destroy enemy naval forces, suppress enemy sea commerce, protect vital sea lanes, and establish local military superiority in vital sea areas. (Approved for incorporation into JP 1-02.)

sea surveillance. None. Approved for removal from JP 1-02.)

service group. None. (Approved for removal from JP 1-02.)

service squadron. None. (Approved for removal from JP 1-02.)

squadron. 1. An organization consisting of two or more divisions of ships, or two or more divisions (Navy) or flights of aircraft. 2. A basic administrative aviation unit of the Army, Navy, Marine Corps, and Air Force. 3. Battalion-sized ground or aviation units. (Approved for incorporation into JP 1-02.)

submarine operating authority. The naval commander exercising operational control of submarines. Also called **SUBOPAUTH.** (Approved for incorporation into JP 1-02 with JP 3-32 as the source JP.)

submarine patrol area. None. (Approved for removal from JP 1-02.)

surface action group. A temporary or standing organization of combatant ships, other than carriers, tailored for a specific tactical mission. Also called **SAG.** (Approved for incorporation into JP 1-02 with JP 3-32 as the source JP.)

surface combatant. A ship constructed and armed for combat use with the capability to conduct operations in multiple maritime roles against air, surface and subsurface threats, and land targets. (Approved for incorporation into JP 1-02 with JP 3-32 as the source JP.)

surface warfare. That portion of maritime warfare in which operations are conducted to destroy or neutralize enemy naval surface forces and merchant vessels. Also called **SUW.** (Approved for incorporation into JP 1-02 with JP 3-32 as the source JP.)

task component. A subdivision of a fleet, task force, task group, or task unit, organized by the respective commander or by higher authority for the accomplishment of specific tasks. (Approved for incorporation into JP 1-02 with JP 3-32 as the source JP.)

task element. A component of a naval task unit organized by the commander of a task unit or higher authority. (Approved for incorporation into JP 1-02 with JP 3-32 as the source JP.)

task force. A component of a fleet organized by the commander of a task fleet or higher authority for the accomplishment of a specific task or tasks. Also called **TF.** (Approved for inclusion in JP 1-02.)

task group. A component of naval task force organized by the commander of a task force or higher authority. Also called **TG.** (Approved for incorporation into JP 1-02 with JP 3-32 as the source JP.)

task unit. A component of a naval task group organized by the commander of a task group or higher authority. (Approved for incorporation into JP 1-02 with JP 3-32 as the source JP.)

theater antisubmarine warfare commander. A Navy commander assigned to develop plans and direct assigned and attached assets for the conduct of antisubmarine warfare within an operational area. Also called **TASWC.** (Approved for incorporation into JP 1-02.)

undersea warfare. Military operations conducted to establish and maintain control of the undersea portion of the maritime domain. Also called **USW.** (Approved for incorporation into JP 1-02.)

waterspace management. The allocation of waterspace in terms of antisubmarine warfare attack procedures to permit the rapid and effective engagement of hostile submarines while preventing inadvertent attacks on friendly submarines. Also called **WSM.** (JP 1-02. SOURCE: JP 3-32)

Intentionally Blank

JOINT DOCTRINE PUBLICATIONS HIERARCHY

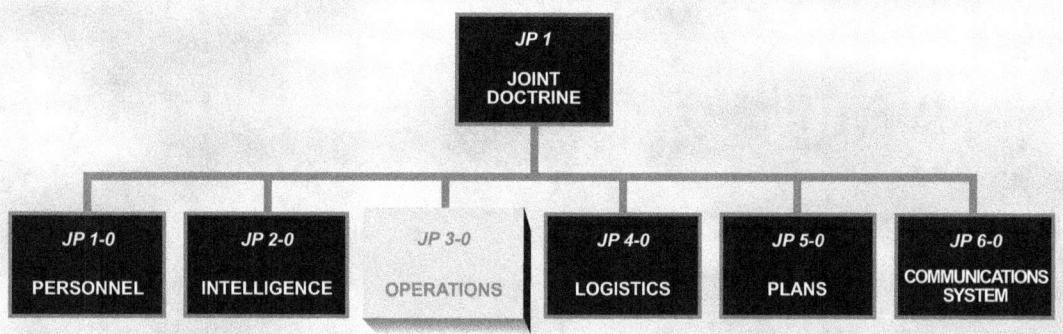

```
                        ┌──────────────┐
                        │     JP 1     │
                        │    JOINT     │
                        │   DOCTRINE   │
                        └──────────────┘
```

JP 1-0	JP 2-0	JP 3-0	JP 4-0	JP 5-0	JP 6-0
PERSONNEL	INTELLIGENCE	OPERATIONS	LOGISTICS	PLANS	COMMUNICATIONS SYSTEM

All joint publications are organized into a comprehensive hierarchy as shown in the chart above. **Joint Publication (JP) 3-32** is in the **Operations** series of joint doctrine publications. The diagram below illustrates an overview of the development process:

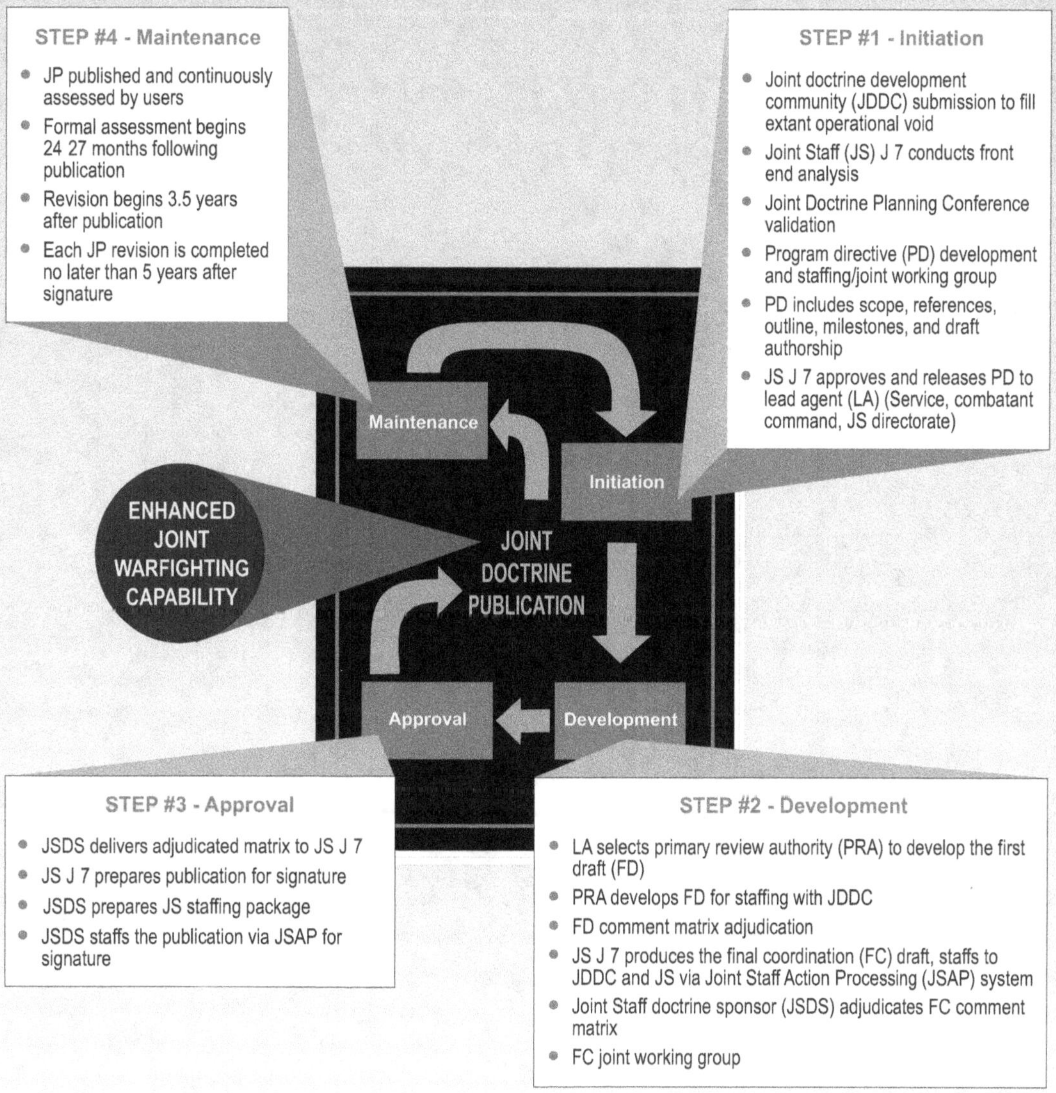

STEP #4 - Maintenance

- JP published and continuously assessed by users
- Formal assessment begins 24 27 months following publication
- Revision begins 3.5 years after publication
- Each JP revision is completed no later than 5 years after signature

STEP #1 - Initiation

- Joint doctrine development community (JDDC) submission to fill extant operational void
- Joint Staff (JS) J 7 conducts front end analysis
- Joint Doctrine Planning Conference validation
- Program directive (PD) development and staffing/joint working group
- PD includes scope, references, outline, milestones, and draft authorship
- JS J 7 approves and releases PD to lead agent (LA) (Service, combatant command, JS directorate)

ENHANCED JOINT WARFIGHTING CAPABILITY

Maintenance — Initiation

JOINT DOCTRINE PUBLICATION

Approval — Development

STEP #3 - Approval

- JSDS delivers adjudicated matrix to JS J 7
- JS J 7 prepares publication for signature
- JSDS prepares JS staffing package
- JSDS staffs the publication via JSAP for signature

STEP #2 - Development

- LA selects primary review authority (PRA) to develop the first draft (FD)
- PRA develops FD for staffing with JDDC
- FD comment matrix adjudication
- JS J 7 produces the final coordination (FC) draft, staffs to JDDC and JS via Joint Staff Action Processing (JSAP) system
- Joint Staff doctrine sponsor (JSDS) adjudicates FC comment matrix
- FC joint working group